The Modernisation Plan
British Railways' Blueprint
for the Future

The Modernisation Plan
British Railways' Blueprint for the Future

David N. Clough

Front cover: Dr Richard Beeching's vision for the future. A 25kV overhead-electric Class 85, No 85033, hauling a down West Coast main line freightliner service at Gayton on 24 June 1976. *John E. Oxley*

First published 2014

ISBN 978 0 7110 3790 8

Published by Ian Allan Publishing

an imprint of Ian Allan Publishing Ltd, Hersham, Surrey KT12 4RG.
Printed in England.

Visit the Ian Allan Publishing website at www.ianallanpublishing.com

Contents

Introduction	9
Chapter 1 The impact of nationalisation	11
Chapter 2 Motive power development 1948-54	21
Chapter 3 Modernising British Railways	37
Chapter 4 The modernisation and re-equipment of British Railways	55
Chapter 5 The Pilot Scheme	65
Chapter 6 Diesel multiple units	79
Chapter 7 Electrification	93
Chapter 8 A journey through design	107
Chapter 9 Inter-city DMUs	111
Chapter 10 Diesel deliveries	125
Chapter 11 Modernisation of train services	145
Chapter 12 Modernisation reappraised	157
Bibliography	169
List of tables	170
Index	171

Contents

Abbreviations

AEI	Associated Electrical Industries
ASLEF	Associated Society of Locomotive Engineers & Firemen
bhp	brake horsepower
Big Four	The four major pre-nationalisation railways
BR	British Railways
BRB	British Railways Board
BRCW	Birmingham Railway Carriage & Wagon Co
BTC	British Transport Commission
BTH	British Thomson Houston
BUT	British United Traction
CM&EE	Chief Mechanical & Electrical Engineer
CRM	Chief Regional Manager (from October 1953)
CRO	Chief Regional Officer (before October 1953)
Commission	BTC
DEMU	Diesel-Electric Multiple Unit
DMU	Diesel (mechanical) Multiple Unit
DRU	Design Research Unit
ECML	East Coast main line
ED	electro-diesel
EE	English Electric Co
EMU	Electric Multiple Unit
ETH	Electric train heating
ER	Eastern Region
GEC	General Electric Company of the UK
GWR	Great Western Railway
KM	Krauss Maffei
LTC	Lightweight Trains Committee
LMR	London Midland Region
LMSR	London Midland & Scottish Railway
LNER	London & North Eastern Railway
LT	London Transport
Metrovick	Metropolitan-Vickers Electrical Co Ltd
mgr	merry-go-round
MoT	Ministry of Transport
NBL	North British Locomotive Co
NCB	National Coal Board
Paxman	Davey Paxman & Co
RE	Railway Executive
rpm	revolutions per minute
ScR	Scottish Region
SR	Southern Region
Southern	Southern Railway
WCML	West Coast main line

Introduction

The modernisation of British Railways is a vast subject. To date, only the diesel locomotive aspects have been discussed to any degree and this book aims to provide much more information about the 1955 Modernisation Plan. With this in mind, it can be seen as complementary to, rather than a duplicate of, my earlier book *Dr Beeching's Remedy – a cure for a century of railway ills*, published in 2013.

It would be tedious to merely list all the schemes undertaken as part of the Plan. Drawing on much previously unpublished official information contained in the British Railways files held within the National Archives, the decision-making processes of some of the major projects are put in the wider context of how a new railway was to be ushered in.

One issue that emerges is the ineptitude of most of the senior railway managers of the 1950s. The breath of reality brought by Richard Beeching and his top-table appointees were the real modernisers, not just of railway hardware, but of the minds of managers who willingly hitched their stars to his wagon.

As the story unfolds there will be surprises along the way, some giving rise to humour and others that question the wisdom of the decision-makers. Above all, it is a tale of how the railways metamorphosed from a system built on 19th-century technology to one that drew on the best that the second half of the 20th century could offer.

For simplicity, the TOPS traction and rolling stock coding has been used throughout, even though this was not introduced until the 1970s.

As always, I am grateful to my wife, Jo, for considerable assistance with research and in proof reading.

David N. Clough
Leigh
January 2014

Chapter 1

The impact of nationalisation

Creating the British Transport Commission

On the nationalisation of the coal industry in 1947, Prime Minister Clement Attlee declared this was part of a great experiment of Socialism within a democracy. His Labour administration had come to power in 1945 and set about taking roughly 20% of the UK economy into public ownership and control.

Whilst experimenting with democratic socialism, the Government faced the major task of repairing damage arising from German bombing during World War 2 and catching up with the arrears of normal repairs, renewals and new investment that had arisen since the onset of war in 1939. Despite full employment, limited Government funds had to be allocated in line with priorities and this meant that an air of austerity prevailed, evidenced by food rationing increasing after hostilities had ended. Whether Attlee's administration appreciated the difficulties that would ensue for Government capital availability within the newly-nationalised industries is not known.

At the annual general meeting of the Great Western Railway in 1947, its chairman said that it was generally accepted that the main transport problem to be addressed was how to achieve a greater measure of co-ordination between various forms of transport, so that public requirements could be best met. He observed that the Transport Bill then before Parliament contained no constructive plan for achieving this. So nationalisation was not viewed purely as an act of political dogma but an attempt at transport co-ordination through State control.

Thus it was that the Transport Act of 1947 ushered in the nationalisation of the railways, road transport (bus and haulage), ports and inland waterways, London Transport and co-ordination of coastal shipping, all within Britain, and created the British Transport Commission (BTC, the Commission) as a public authority to carry out these activities.

Sir Cyril Hurcomb, who had been the Permanent Secretary (most senior civil servant) at the Ministry of Transport during the passage of the Transport Bill and was later ennobled, was appointed BTC Chairman. The transfer of the privately-owned businesses came into effect on 1 January 1948. Hurcomb would have spent his working life close in, or close to, Westminster and the seat of

Government. Perhaps for this reason the Commission set up its headquarters in London Transport's offices at 51 Broadway, which is over St James's Park underground station and within walking distance of the Houses of Parliament.

Provision was made in Part 1, Section 5, of the Act for the creation of executive bodies to administer, maintain and operate the Commission's activities and the Railway Executive (RE) fulfilled this function for British Railways (BR). It was a public authority in its own right, by far the largest constituent within the Commission, and acted as the BTC's agent in fulfilling its duties, which were laid down by the Commission and approved by the Minister of Transport. Members of the RE were appointed by the Minister after consultation with the Commission.

The RE was organised on functional lines, with each full-time member being both a member of the Executive and having specific Departmental responsibility. Appointments to these posts were announced by the Minister on 12 September 1947 and were as follows:

Function	Appointee
Chairman	Sir Eustace Missenden (ex General Manager, Southern Railway)
Publicity, public relations, estates and rating, police, stores	Gen Sir William Slim (ex Army)
Staff and establishment, welfare, medical	W. P. Allen (General Secretary ASLEF, previously driver Great Northern Railway)
Railway operating, marine, docks	V. M. Barrington-Ward (Divisional General Manager London & North Eastern Railway)
Commercial, passenger, goods, mineral, cartage, Continental	David Blee (Chief Goods Manager, Great Western Railway)
Mechanical engineering, electrical engineering, road motor engineering, scientific research	R. A. Riddles (Vice President, London Midland & Scottish Railway)
Civil and dock engineering, signalling and telecommunications, architecture	J. C. L. Train (Chief Engineer, London & North Eastern Railway)

General Slim resigned in November 1948 on promotion to Chief of the Imperial General Staff and he was succeeded in 1949 by General Sir Daril Watson. Missenden assumed functional responsibility for publicity and public relations.

The RE organisation also included a Chief Legal Adviser and Solicitor and a Chief Financial Officer. Within their functions, Members were supported by Chief Officers and these collectively formed the RE headquarters organisation, based at 222 Marylebone Road, the former Great Central Hotel attached to the station. It is worth quoting from the BTC's annual report for 1948 to see how the RE's structure was described: '. . . in setting up the organisation the Executive endeavoured particularly to avoid the creation of an over-centralised organisation at the top'. Meanwhile, 'the detailed supervision, maintenance and operation of the railway system should be vested in departmental officers in six Regions'. In the light of events, many would disagree with this aspiration.

The Regions were drawn up based largely on routes of the pre-nationalisation Big Four railways with some modification. A new Scottish Region (ScR) included all routes in Scotland, the London Midland (LMR) got the ex-LMSR routes in England, the North Eastern (NER) and Eastern (ER) were made up of the LNER's English routes divided at Leeds and Doncaster, the Western (WR) and Southern (SR) were the former GWR and Southern Railway routes respectively. In drawing up the RE's structure and Regions, the BTC was mindful to minimise drastic changes to well-tried organisations and long-established practices.

The RE's functional structure, as set out above, was replicated at Regional level and the latter reported to the relevant Chief Officer at HQ. A Chief Regional Manager (CRM) in each Region reported directly to the Executive and was responsible for the general administration of the Region within the policy and general instructions of the Executive. The CRM also co-ordinated the work of Regional departmental officers and handled local recruitment but this post was nowhere near as powerful as the General Manager in each of the four pre-nationalisation railways.

Investment
By 1947, the pre-nationalisation Big Four railway companies were in a position to begin a programme of capital investment; in fact Sir Ronald Matthews, LNER Chairman, referred to this in his annual address. Just a year later, State control presented a rather different state of affairs. Again, it is worth referring to the BTC's annual report for 1948.

Whilst there were aspirations for development, economic stringency and recovery from war damage meant attention be confined to reconstruction and reconditioning. The Commission did not feel the time was right to even compile a programme for capital development (investment aimed at renewal on an enhancement basis, rather than repair). 'The chief objective of the Commission must perforce be to make the best possible use of such resources as can be made available for rehabilitation schemes.' A Government-wide Investment Programmes Committee reviewed the plans for all Central Government bodies and this encompassed not only capital projects but also the 'investment' in the renewal and maintenance of physical works.

Such funds as could be squeezed out of the Treasury were largely absorbed by the Commission's commitment to continue with schemes put in hand before nationalisation. These schemes included:

- Electrification of the Manchester, Sheffield and Wath route and a new tunnel at Woodhead;
- Electrification between Liverpool Street and Shenfield;
- Remodelling of Potters Bar station (phase 1);
- Reconstruction of platforms at Portsmouth Harbour station;
- Mechanisation of the foundry at Horwich Locomotive Works;
- New carriage shops at Doncaster Works;
- Facilities for repair of locomotives and wagons at St Rollox Works;
- Colour light signalling at Battersea Park and Bricklayers Arms Junction to Coulsdon North;
- Reconstruction of Southall Motive Power Depot;
- Operating facilities for ICI at Grangetown;
- New ocean passenger terminal at Southampton;
- New carriage shed and sidings at Willesden, north London;
- Mechanisation of the Up marshalling yard at Toton.

So this was one impact of democratic socialism not mentioned by the politicians. The BTC was in a political pecking order and up against education and health for what could be afforded, rather than the railways being free to spend whatever they could afford, as appertained before nationalisation. This, of course, was to be a recurring theme down to railway privatisation in the 1990s.

It will be helpful for the time being to stay with the topic of investment, as viewed through the Commission's annual reports, because this builds the picture of what was to come later with the Modernisation Plan.

The biggest scheme in progress was electrification of the Woodhead route between Manchester London Road (later Piccadilly), Sheffield Victoria, Rotherwood Yard and Wath. It was a project inherited from the LNER and some equipment had been procured and then stored at the outbreak of the war. Electrification was to the 1,500V DC system supplied through an overhead line. According to the 1949 report, 85 locomotives and 24 coaches were to be constructed; in fact, 57 'EM1' (later Class 76) and seven 'EM2' (later Class 77) electrics were built.

Staying with electrification, in January 1949 the RE brought together a team to start work on plans to electrify the London, Tilbury & Southend line. Electrification between London and Shenfield was opened on 26 September, though delivery of the 92 three-car EMUs was delayed due to a shortage of labour and materials.

The 1949 report stated that the BTC's programme of development to make good deficiencies in physical assets was affected adversely by a shortage of steel and a reduction in the level of capital investment imposed by the Government. One million tons of steel was required for renewals (including the replacement of wooden-bodied wagons) but only 810,000 tons was made available. Track replacement totalled 2,000 tons, of which 1,365 were for new rails.

If the Commission had been hamstrung thus far in its development and investment plans, 1950 was even worse. Sterling had been devalued in autumn 1949 and the BTC had to fight hard to keep the value of the Government's cut in money for investment to 8%; rising costs in industry added to the problem. The reduction in capital expenditure cut the number of locomotives built from a planned 466 to 391 in 1949 and 436 to 411 in 1950.

Yet another example of how publicly-owned undertakings can be buffeted by national events in a way that their privately-owned counterparts would not can be seen from the opening sentence in the BTC's 1951 report. It referred to the general economic background that year being affected by rearmament, under which the Government would be allocating an increased share of its funds towards the military and away from civilian activities. In that year the Government had made available £81 million for capital projects within the RE and London Transport but only £76.1 million had been able to be spent due to shortages of labour, steel and non-ferrous metals. Construction of locomotives was 340 against a programme of 447, whilst 1,923 new coaches represented a shortfall of 841.

1952 brought no respite for the BTC and the opening sentence in its annual report for that year states that the Government continued to exercise control over capital investment. In hindsight, it is remarkable that the Commission chose to open its review of the year with such a statement. Limits of £76.6 million and

£7.2 million were set for BR and LT respectively and, in the Commission's words, the restrictions on investment since 1948 had forced a 'make do and mend' approach that was not cost-effective.

Modernisation projects that had been sanctioned were, however, making progress. On 4 February the first phase of electric traction was introduced on the Manchester, Sheffield and Wath scheme and covered the Wath to Barnsley Junction section. The whole scheme was finished in 1954.

The Railway Electrification Committee held meetings in 1948, 1949 and 1950. It reaffirmed the earlier decision for a national standard system of 1,500V DC but recommended a trial using an AC 50-cycles supply, both being via overhead line. The former Midland Railway route between Lancaster, Morecambe and Heysham was selected for this trial because it had been electrified on the overhead system by the Midland Railway in 1908. The latest scheme used 6,600V AC and the first three-car EMU started running in November 1952. Whilst there were (not insurmountable) problems with interference to telecommunications, overall the experiment was judged to be a success.

Another gloomy position regarding new investment was described in the 1953 annual report. Across the whole of the Commission's undertakings, only £68 million had been spent and this was not even catching up on the railways with arrears of maintenance accrued during World War 2. 'The shortage of steel and other materials; the inadequate supply of engineering technicians; and the discouraging and disrupting effects of constantly changing limits upon capital investment have all combined to hinder progress.' Quite a side-swipe at the attitude of Government! The report goes on to say it had been possible to do little beyond continuing with major projects started before the war, such as Manchester, Sheffield and Wath electrification.

With optimism for the future, the report commented that the BTC's capital asset needs had been clearly assessed and several important lines of development were in hand. It was hoped that the era of severely-restricted technical betterment was ending. Perhaps the largest new project to be sanctioned was the widening to four tracks of the East Coast main line (ECML) between New Barnet and Potters Bar. Electrification schemes at various stages of consideration included Liverpool Street to Enfield and Chingford, King's Cross outer suburban and reactivation of the Southern Railway's 1946 plans for all routes east of a line drawn between Reading and Portsmouth. Since the 1953 report was written during 1954, the notes of optimism for the future are interesting.

Transport Act 1953
A downside of being a nationalised industry is to make it exposed to shifts in the political colour of the Government. The general election in 1950 returned Labour to power but with a small majority and it was necessary to hold a fresh election the following year, which resulted in a Conservative victory with Winston Churchill as Prime Minister. Whilst no attempt was made to return the railways to private ownership, a Transport Act in 1953 did result in changes to the BTC.

The objects of this Act were broadly to:

- Return the bulk of the British Road Services fleet to private ownership.
- Abolish the 25-mile restriction on private hauliers.
- Revoke exemption of the Commission's vehicles from licensing regulations.
- Set up a transport levy to meet the Commission's capital loss on disposals plus £1 million 'disturbance' loss.
- Abolish the Hotels, Road Transport and Docks & Inland Waterways Executives and set up new control arrangements.
- Abolish the Railway Executive and decentralise control to Area Boards and the Regions.

It also repealed the provisions contained in the 1947 Act for setting up area schemes for road passenger transport and for trade harbours. The intention of the 1947 Act was that neither the BTC nor the various Executives would wield undue centralising control but this had turned out to be far from the case.

From 1 October 1953 the primary function of the BTC was to be the control of major policy, including finance and general direction. Commission Members were not supposed to be equivalent to a board of directors, yet full-time Members *were* now effectively heads of disciplines.

Lord Hurcomb retired as the Commission's chairman on 31 August 1953 and it is interesting to note that he was not succeeded by anyone with even remote links to transport, or anyone from the world of business or commerce, but by General Sir Brian Robertson. The latter did not arrive back in the UK from a posting in Egypt until November 1953 and claimed that the Prime Minister had instructed him to give the railways leadership. To a degree, this ran counter to the decentralisation policy of the Act, albeit ill-defined therein.

The 1953 Act left unresolved the matter of control of the railways and further legislation was enacted in 1954 to deal with this. For some reason, the 1953 Act had used the word Area, not Region, and this carried through into the 1954 provisions, which created Area Boards, one for each Region. In essence the Area Boards supervised the Chief Regional Managers (formerly the Chief Regional Officers and hereinafter Regional Managers), who now ran the railways on a day-to-day basis; they attended Commission meetings but were not Members.

Board tasks were top-level management akin to those of directors, promoting initiative in improving services and facilities, liaison with users, and monitoring of health and safety. A key function was to be the setting and monitoring of revenue and capital budgets, subject to over-riding BTC scrutiny. The Commission left it to each Board to decide where and how frequently they would meet and how they would conduct their business. Area Boards came into being on 1 January 1955 and started work on 1 February.

Area Board members were to be 'wise men of light and learning' and who had contact with commerce, industry and labour but not representatives of trade or other sectional interests. So what calibre were these members? By way of example, the Eastern Area Board comprised a BTC member (as chairman), the Lord Lieutenant of Norfolk who had agricultural interests, the vice-chairman of Northern Rubber Ltd, a former president of the Amalgamated Union of Engineers, a member of the Committee of Enquiry into the electricity industry and finally a member of Magdalen College, Cambridge.

Turning now to the restructuring of the Commission, interim arrangements were put in place until Robertson arrived and for convenience this will be referred to here as the interim structure. Some changes were made to Commission membership, with Langdale Train promoted from the RE and A. B. B. Valentine from London Transport; Train thus became the most senior engineer in the Commission. The RE's Member for mechanical and electrical engineering, R. A. Riddles, chose to retire, rather than seek a post in the new hierarchy. Frank Pope had already joined the BTC from the chair of the Ulster Transport Authority, having previously been a Vice President of the LMSR. His area of responsibility now covered commercial and operational affairs. Other Commission Members had backgrounds in the trade unions, accountancy, the Civil Service and industry and commerce.

Robertson was given a Ministerial free hand in drawing up an organisation for the BTC headquarters. This developed during 1954 into a fiendishly complex structure. Commission members operated through sub-commissions and committees and the former comprised one for each area of the BTC. Below this level were the BTC Divisions, viz, British Railways Central Staff, British Road Services (formerly the Road Transport Executive), Road Passenger companies, British Transport Docks, British Transport Waterways and British Transport Hotels & Catering.

Pope and Train were among the Members who served on the sub-commission for railways. Committees were function-based and dealt with the day-to-day running of the Commission. Each committee was chaired by a Commission Member and was attended by a General Staff Adviser, Chief Officers from the HQ Divisions and BR Regional Managers, as appropriate. Where relevant or necessary (for example, approval of expenditure above a prescribed amount), these committees made recommendations to the Commission for a final decision.

Two of these committees are pertinent to railway modernisation, the Works & Equipment Committee (hereinafter referred to as the Works Committee) and the Technical, Research & Development Committee (hereinafter referred to as the Technical Committee). The Works Committee dealt with all expenditure above the level delegated to the BTC Area Boards and was chaired by Pope whilst Train ran the Technical Committee.

As an HQ Division, the BR Central Staff was organised by function, with each being headed by a Chief Officer. The disciplines comprised Commercial, Motive Power & Operating, Establishment and Staff, Mechanical Engineering, Carriage & Wagon Engineering, Electrical Engineering, Civil Engineering, Signal Engineering, Finance and finally Research. R. C. Bond was Chief Mechanical Engineer, whilst under the October 1953 interim structure John Ratter was the Chief Civil Engineer. The Central Staff supported the work of their masters, who were the Commission Members, and had direct access to their counterparts in the Regions. This made, for example, the WR's Chief Mechanical Engineer accountable to both his Regional Manager and the Central Staff.

The first HQ appointment made by Robertson was that of General Sir Daril Watson as Secretary-General; as an RE Member his remit had covered publicity, public relations, estates and rating, police and stores. On his retirement in 1955 he was succeeded by another Army retiree, Major-General L. Wansbrough-Jones. The latter's salary was £4,000, £1,000 less than Watson had been paid.

Watson headed up a secretariat, which was called the General Staff, whose role was co-ordination of all Commission activity. It therefore provided assistance to the sub-commissions and committees. Senior officers within the General Staff were given the title of Adviser and their duties related to matters of policy and to ensure consistency of action in matters of principle and in the settlement of Regional and inter-Regional questions. Standardisation and consistency of approach had been one benefit brought about through nationalisation. Advisers' posts within the General Staff comprised Financial Administration, Chief Solicitor and Legal Adviser, Traffic Adviser, Chief Secretary, Chief of General Duties, Manpower Adviser, Technical Adviser,

Supplies & Production Adviser and (from 1955) the Public Relations Adviser.

Former RE Members David Blee and W. P. Allen were the Traffic and Manpower Advisers respectively, whose salaries were the same as Watson's, even though now subordinate to him. These Adviser posts were not part of the initial post-October 1953 Commission structure and may have been created for, in particular, former RE Members who had not been given (in their eyes) a sufficiently senior job; Blee was a case in point. Ratter took the post of Technical Adviser from Chief Officer Civil Engineering within the BR Central Staff. When Train retired from the Commission, Ratter replaced him and Bond became Technical Adviser, so this perhaps gives a clue to the pecking order.

Commentators at the time viewed the above Commission structure as top-heavy and centralising. Terry Gourvish, a professor at Essex University who was officially commissioned to write a business history of BR, commented that 'the supposed functions of the new General Staff elude precise definition', whilst the precise roles of the Divisions (such as the BR Central Staff) were left 'rather vague'. Readers struggling to get to grips with the structure are therefore in good company! It is unsurprising that Dr Richard Beeching swept all this away when he became BTC chairman in 1961. Nevertheless, an understanding of this structure and the key personnel involved will help with a better appreciation of later events.

A side effect of the post-1953 structure was the call made on staff time attending meetings in London. This can be illustrated by a point made by the ScR Regional Manager that 90 return first class sleeper berths were reserved every week for senior Regional staff travelling back and forth to London on business.

With Hurcomb gone, the Commission joined the RE at 222 Marylebone Road. Finally, a spirit of competition was now to exist between British Road Services and BR. The latter had seen its rates and charges fixed by Government for political purposes, rather than based on any reflection of rising costs. Whilst this largely remained the case, the railways were given some latitude in order to compete with road transport. Here it becomes clear how the shifting political sand dune had removed the BTC's role as the co-ordinating body for transport enshrined in the 1947 Act in favour of competition.

Chapter 2

Motive power development 1948-54

Personalities and politics
In 1946 a delegation of senior locomotive engineers from Britain, including Arthur Peppercorn, the CM&EE of the LNER, visited the USA. There they found development work on steam traction had effectively ended; the emphasis was now on diesel motive power. In postwar western Europe the extensive and expensive reconstruction of national infrastructure, notably the railways, moved in favour of electrification for main lines or diesel power for secondary routes.

In 1948 the BTC asked that a committee of non-engineers be set up to look at alternatives to steam on economic grounds, so even they were alive to the changing face of railway operation. Despite all this, only in Britain did the steam locomotive continue to be viewed as the way forward by those within the Railway Executive with responsibility for such matters.

R. A. Riddles was the RE Member for mechanical and electrical engineering, the CM&EE in common parlance. His view on motive power was to retain steam until electrification could be afforded. E. S. Cox, whom Riddles appointed to head rolling stock design, said the decision to continue with steam happened by default 'because the steam interests were all set to jump in with the utmost vigour, whereas a certain amount of fact finding was necessary for other forms of traction'. He added that other RE Members either concurred or did not oppose this approach.

It is against this background that events over the period under review in this chapter should be judged.

Alternatives to steam before 1948
Railway companies had been looking at alternative forms of motive power since the 19th century. Electrification had been chosen for underground lines, such as those in London and Liverpool. Overground, the Southern had opted for a third-rail system and both the North Eastern and Lancashire & Yorkshire (L&YR) Railways had converted lines on Tyneside and on Merseyside and in North Manchester respectively to this form of traction. In 1913 the L&YR's Bury to

Holcombe Brook branch had been electrified using overhead line supply, rather than via a third rail.

In 1931 the Government set up the Weir Committee to examine future main line traction options and its report came down in favour of electrification of all such routes as the most economical, using an overhead line supply at 1,500V DC. This became the national standard and was used in the various schemes drawn up by the LNER.

All these, and a number of others, were passenger suburban operations and the first main line scheme comprised the LNER's Manchester, Sheffield and Wath route where freight predominated over passenger. Work on this stalled in 1939 with the onset of war and was reactivated at the end of hostilities in 1945. What is not generally known is that the GWR had drawn up plans in 1938 to electrify its main line over the South Devon banks west of Newton Abbot; this also stalled with the onset of hostilities. After the war, the LNER began to plan for electrification of the southern end of its ECML.

Use of the internal combustion engine first employed petrol until serious fires in the aftermath of accidents made it clear that this fuel was too dangerous for the rail environment. Fresh trials came when the diesel engine became a practical form of rail propulsion from the 1920s. Power plants of varying sizes were tried out in, or under, locomotives for main-line use, but primarily for shunting work and railcars.

Of particular note was the decision of the LMSR to opt for diesel traction as its future standard shunting locomotive. It also experimented with railcars, one design that emerged in 1938 being the prototype of the modern DMU in coupling three underfloor-powered vehicles together. The GWR built a series of railcars for suburban, branch line and even inter-city duties.

After the war both the LMSR and Southern decided to build prototype diesel locomotives for evaluation. Of these, only one, No 10000, emerged prior to nationalisation.

No 10000, and its sister No 10001, were sometimes described by the LMSR in the singular because the intention had been to use both in multiple as a single traction unit. They were identical mechanically and had an English Electric Co (EE) powertrain, comprising an EE 16SVT 16-cylinder diesel of 1,600bhp output at 750rpm, coupled to which was an EE main generator. Power was fed to six EE traction motors, one each mounted on the two three-axle bogies. When paired together, the combined traction unit could perform any of the duties diagrammed for the largest LMSR '8P' Pacific steam types. As individual machines, they were classed as medium power and put in quite a lot of mileage on the LMR in the early 1950s on freight turns because their steam train heating equipment was unreliable.

The LMSR also ordered a diesel-electric of quite low power from the North British Locomotive Co (NBL). Whereas Nos 10000/1 had a driving cab at each end, No 10800 was very similar to an American 'road switcher' in having just one cab. Starting at one end, there was the cooler group (radiators and radiator fan). Next came the power plant (engine and generator set) and train heating boiler. A single cab followed this, with a stub nose at the other end that contained the control cubicle. Locating the cab in this way gave better bi-directional visibility than by having a single cab at one end.

Two four-wheel bogies, each with two powered axles, carried the body. Davey Paxman & Co (Paxman) supplied its RPH model of diesel in 16-cylinder form and this developed 827bhp at 1,250rpm. The engine drove electrical machines of British Thomson Houston (BTH) manufacture. No 10800 was intended for duties on branch and secondary lines.

No 10100 was a collaboration between the LMR, Fell Developments Ltd and Shell Petroleum, though it seems likely that initial discussions pre-dated nationalisation. Lt Col L. F. R. Fell devised the concept for this sole example of a main line diesel-mechanical traction unit. Shell provided funding for the project and H. G. Ivatt, the LMR's CME, facilitated matters and made Derby Works available for design and construction.

Conceptually, No 10100 was a 4-8-4 or 2D2, with nose ends and two driving cabs. A further change from normal practice was locating the main propulsion engines in the nose ends. These were four 12RHP Paxman diesels, each rated at 500bhp at 1,500rpm. A diesel-mechanical system aimed to eliminate the internal losses in both diesel-electric and diesel-hydraulic propulsion, whereby only between 75 to 80% of engine power was actually available at the wheel rim. Secondly, there was a multi-engined arrangement that drove through slip couplings and differential gears. Finally a variable boost was applied to the engines so that a high boost at low speed produced high torque, with reduced boost at high speed.

No 10100 emerged from Derby in 1950 but suffered several severe failures during its eight-year life. It had a top speed of 78mph and trials confirmed the predicted performance characteristics of high transmission efficiency. By the date of its last major crippling incident, a steam generator fire in 1958, the world of diesel traction had moved on and No 10100 failed to make any impact on the future of BR's motive power policy.

Finally, there were the Southern's main line prototypes. Although started before 1948, these did not emerge until after nationalisation. The first two,

Nos 10201/2, were fitted with a very similar power train to Nos 10000/1, namely an EE 16SVT diesel and EE main generator and traction motors; technical development, however, saw the engine rated at 1,750bhp at 750rpm.

The axle load limit was set at 18 tons for two reasons. First, the Southern had considerable experience of the effect that small-wheeled bogies, with axle-hung traction motors, had on damaging the track. Reducing the axle load would lessen the track stresses. Secondly, a low axle load offered greater route availability and so more operational flexibility. Unlike the LMSR machines, therefore, the Southern's CME, O. V. S. Bulleid, designed a four-axle bogie to spread the weight of the locomotive, though the leading axle on each bogie was unpowered.

The duo appeared in 1950 and 1951 respectively and were used on services to Exeter initially and also Bournemouth from Waterloo. They were joined in 1952 by Nos 10000/1 and 10800 from the LMR. Operationally, their records were blighted by long periods out of traffic, partly due to design flaws in equipment, possibly waiting for spare parts, possibly due to disinterest in allocating staff time to carry out the work. A further prototype, No 10203, entered traffic in 1954 and was mechanically similar to its Southern sisters. It benefited from a version of EE's 16SVT diesel which was now rated at 2,000bhp at 850rpm.

Once the SR had decided not to proceed with main line diesel traction, preferring to retain steam until its Wessex and West of England routes could be electrified, the six prototypes moved to the LMR were they saw out their days. One BR report in 1954 judged them a success in terms of on-the-road performance and potential utilisation. By contrast, another report judged them as failures because of the long periods spent out of service. Typical average annual mileages of 80,000 compare favourably to SR steam performance and, indeed, that of BR's large diesels during the 1960s and 1970s.

In 1946 the GWR ordered a gas-turbine powered locomotive, No 18000, from British Brown-Boveri Ltd, with construction at its works at Baden, Switzerland, in conjunction with the Swiss Locomotive & Machine Works, Winterthur, Switzerland. The latter was responsible for the mechanical parts, which comprised, essentially, the bogies, the main frame and the superstructure. After allowing for the power absorbed by the 7,500hp compressor, the 10,000hp turbine was able to supply 2,500hp input to a main generator. Output from the generator was supplied to four traction motors, which were mounted on the outer axles of two bogies. A third axle on each bogie was used for weight distribution.

Delivery was in 1950. Although geared for a 90mph top speed, the four traction motors were only rated at a combined 1,680hp, which meant a low transmission efficiency of 67% as opposed to around 80% for a diesel-electric locomotive. Whilst on normal duties, thermal efficiency was also little better than a steam locomotive and this showed up the fundamental flaw of the gas turbine when working at below 80% of output.

Also in 1946, the GWR entered into a collaboration with the Metropolitan-Vickers Electrical Co Ltd (Metrovick) for the design, building, testing and operation of a gas-turbine locomotive, with the costs to be borne equally. To handle the heaviest passenger trains at high speed, an available turbine output of 3,000hp was chosen and in order to absorb the current produced by the main generator which the turbine powered, six traction motors were fitted, one per axle on the two bogies. Numbered No 18100, delivery came in 1951 but the locomotive quickly proved to be very fuel-thirsty and was put to one side in 1953.

No 18000 lasted until 1959 when damage caused by equipment left on the track was not repaired. Gas turbine propulsion has been tried a number of times subsequently overseas, as well as in BR's Advanced Passenger Train prototype, but the issue of thermal efficiency at rates of operation well below full power has never been resolved.

Unquestionably the most unusual locomotive inherited by BR from the pre-nationalisation companies was the Southern's 'Leader' class of coal-fired 0-6-6-0 tanks. Of the five ordered in 1947, only No 36001 was completed. Bulleid tried to design a steam engine that addressed issues of servicing that were becoming an increasing problem after the war. The design looked more like a diesel or electric by virtue of having a cab at each end and being mounted on two bogies. Conceived for heavy shunting and trip freight duties, the design was overtaken by nationalisation, when Bulleid left BR and the RE's mechanical engineers were disinterested in devoting time, effort and money to the project. In fact, it has been alleged that the RE fiddled the trial running results to demonstrate failure, whereas those involved with the project on the SR maintained the 'Leader' class had potential.

In 1941 the Southern introduced the first of three prototype DC electric locomotives, the others following in 1945 and 1948. These were hybrids in that they employed the standard Southern third-rail current collection system but also had a pantograph for overhead supply in yards and a flywheel to cope with gaps in the third rail. Numbered Nos 20001-3 by BR, they were used on passenger services such as the Victoria to Newhaven boat train and freight duties. Traction equipment was of EE manufacture.

The LNER had decided to electrify its trans-Pennine Woodhead route in 1936 and in 1939 Metrovick had been awarded an order for power equipment for 70 locomotives that were to be built at Doncaster. Due to the onset of hostilities, only No 6701 was built in 1940 and taken into LNER stock the following year. It had little opportunity to run because of a lack of electrified routes and was loaned to Netherlands Railways after the war for this purpose. This assisted in refining the design that was then replicated as Class EM1 (Class 76 under BR's later classification) on the Woodhead route.

Cost/benefit of steam after 1948

On nationalisation the RE took over some 20,000 steam locomotives of 448 designs. One view was that Britain had plentiful stocks of coal and no oil, so steam was the logical choice for post-nationalisation motive power renewal. In fact, postwar, there was a shortage of good locomotive coal because a significant proportion of what was being mined was going for export. To address this, the Government pushed the railways to convert locomotives in discrete areas (Cornwall was one) to oil instead of coal. Within a short time, it was appreciated that the nation lacked the foreign currency to buy oil from overseas and the scheme was abandoned, with the costs of conversion wasted. The rationing of fuel oil continued until 1953.

In typical Government fashion, a Working Party on Locomotive Coal was set up by the MoT and this found that 62.6 pounds of coal was being burned per engine-mile in 1951, as opposed to 52.5 pounds in 1938. This was attributed to postwar vagaries in coal quality, though statistical accuracy for such a broad-brush average and the competence of inexperienced firemen might have also been factors.

Postwar Britain was a place of full employment. Jobs associated with steam locomotives were relatively poorly paid and dirty. Of course BR was heavily unionised and had strong lines of trade demarcation and this reflected on the number of personnel employed in motive power depots. It is illuminating to delineate the breadth of different trades involved in an 'X' exam, which was performed every 12 to 16 days on a steam locomotive:

a fire dropper,
a boilersmith and his mate,
an examining fitter,
a cooler-down,
a tube sweeper,

a barman,
a washer-out and his mate,
fitters,
a steam raiser.

Some of these jobs were filthy and inside the firebox where access was difficult. Unsurprisingly, recruitment to some of these trades, and to the job of locomotive cleaner, was a struggle, particularly where better-paid alternatives were available. Reference has been made earlier to a shift away from steam in virtually all western countries after 1945 and the issues of coal and labour supply should have weighed in motive power planning on BR. In truth, these factors did but only within a steam-focused policy.

Concern that RE policy in this area seemed to be blind-siding alternatives started by the decision in April 1948 to mount a series of trials involving locomotives from the four former railway companies. According to Cox, the trials were more for psychological than technical reasons, in order to demonstrate that any modern locomotive could work on any Region. This was aimed at dispelling longstanding beliefs that engines from one Region were bespoke for the traffic demands of its home territory. It seems beyond comprehension that qualified engineers at the top of their profession could hold such beliefs, assuming Cox was right and they did!

The types selected were from power classifications '8P' (the largest express passenger), '5MT' (middle-power mixed traffic) and '7F' or '8F' (heavy freight). Each Region chose the actual locomotive to be used and this was sent with a footplate crew to the other Regions in order to operate on normal diagrammed work but with a dynamometer car to measure performance.

Despite Cox's assertion, in hindsight this exercise was little more than boys playing trains and Cox admits much pleasure was obtained from the circus. It could be argued that it was sensible to opine on what constituted the best design features but that did not need running ex-LNER 'A4s' to Plymouth or Southern Light Pacifics to Inverness! The trials did not uncover why the 'A4' boiler was not always a good steam-raiser, something the home Region knew because its first choice representative from the class was one of only a few which had a double chimney. The trials found that the Light Pacifics were heavy on coal but did not show how to reduce consumption. Aspects of design, such as having a rocking grate to ease disposal at depots, did not need expensive trials to establish. Conducting the trials sent a clear signal that the RE planned to continue to develop the steam locomotive for the foreseeable future.

Hard on the heels of the announcement of (what were known as) the Locomotive Exchanges came news that the RE intended to build 12 new 'Standard' designs of steam locomotive, six of which would be in the 1951 Building Programme. Cox's proposal for these designs was dated 14 June.

Seemingly the RE had already decided on the key features of these designs in so far it had determined power classifications and wheel arrangements. Riddles,

Bond and Cox were all LMSR men and the key elements of most of the Standard classes were based on an equivalent from that railway. In fairness, these were as good as any from other members of the Big Four. Locomotives built in the early 1950s would have a planned operating life of between 30 to 40 years, which would envisage steam on BR continuing well into the 1980s.

On learning of the announcement of the Locomotive Exchanges, Michael Bonavia (who rose in 1954 to become the Chief Officer [New Works] in the BTC) drafted a letter for the Commission to send to the RE enquiring about its motive power policy. This was signed by the Commission's chairman in April 1948 and suggested that a committee should be appointed, which should include a representative of the BTC, to report on the estimated future balance of advantages as between steam and other forms of motive power. The letter recommended that the committee should not be composed of engineers but should gather information from all necessary sources, both inside and outside the Commission.

Design work on the proposed Standard types continued throughout 1948 but it was not until December, eight months after Hurcomb's letter to the RE, that a committee was formed. This was chaired by J. L. Harrington, the RE's Chief Officer (Administration), but pointedly ignored the inclusion of a BTC representative. The committee finally delivered its report in October 1951 and made several recommendations:

- Diesel traction should be used for shunting at all appropriate locations.
- A scheme for the electrification of the Great Northern (out of King's Cross) should be commenced immediately.
- A main line trial in a discrete area of 100 diesel locomotives of 2,000bhp.
- A scheme for a fleet of modern diesel railcars.

Before the Harrington Committee reported, also in 1951 the WR produced its own review of the ex-GWR railcars. These were in use on suburban, branch and cross-country lines and even operated a premium rate inter-city service between Birmingham and Cardiff; dedicated vehicles to convey parcels had also been built. The findings were that these vehicles had been a success and the concept was worth further development. Why had it been left for the WR to conduct such a review, rather than Riddles' Department?

The Harrington Committee's report accepted that steam would be around for many years but that there was no prospect of removing its inherent disadvantages and limitations. By way of response, the RE ignored the proposals for the trial of main line diesel traction on cost grounds and the GN electrification.

At its meeting on 1 November 1951, it proposed a five-phase programme from 1953 for the construction of 573 350hp and 141 150-200hp diesel shunters. The RE also set up a Lightweight Trains Committee to examine that proposal and a report was delivered in March 1952. As regards the trial of 2,000hp main line diesels, Cox explains the lack of implementation was down to two factors. First, the Labour Government that had nationalised transport had been replaced by a Conservative administration and the RE suspected its days were numbered. In consequence it did not want to make long-term plans for electrification. Secondly, Riddles was against the idea because he did not envisage an intermediate phase between steam and full electrification.

Of course, construction of Riddles' new BR Standard types continued apace. These were to incorporate features to assist depot maintenance and locomotive preparation by footplate crews. In short, the new Standards would have all 'mod cons' but would still be a thermally-inefficient, labour-intensive and heavily-polluting form of traction.

Clearly the BTC was disappointed at the way the RE had handled this whole affair, which had begun nearly four years earlier. Bonavia asserts that this was a key factor in the decision to abolish the RE in the 1953 Transport Act.

Smoke and dirt associated with steam power was becoming an issue in London in particular at this time and London County Council began to press for its elimination from the capital. The Eastern Region's electrification schemes were not primarily aimed at addressing this because they appertained only to suburban passenger traffic but they did at least help.

Faced with Railway Executive recalcitrance, the BTC set up its own committee to consider the policy to be adopted for railway motive power, taking account of the need to provide an efficient public service and to make it pay; Bonavia was the secretary. F. A. Pope, who had been a Vice-President of the LMSR along with Riddles, had recently joined the BTC as a Member from the chair of the Ulster Transport Authority, where he had seen the benefits accruing from the use of railcars. The group reported in April 1952, considerably more quickly than Harrington's RE committee, and recommended:

- Support for the Harrington Committee recommendation for an extensive trial of large diesel locomotives.
- The development of the use of diesel railcars or light trains.
- Major main line schemes of electrification should not be proposed due to the severe restrictions on capital investment and extensions to existing schemes were a better prospect.

Cox admits that it was Pope who drove through the lightweight railcar programme, despite adversities; Cox does not say whether these included adversaries too! By 1954 new construction of branch passenger steam types was wound down.

Steam locomotive construction

Having set out the political and strategic background for the motive power policy pursued by the RE after nationalisation, it is worth looking at what actually transpired.

As with the orders for non-steam traction, with three exceptions the RE honoured commitments placed by the pre-nationalisation railways. According to Cox, if an existing design was suitable for the planned allocation, its construction was justifiable over a Standard alternative. Perhaps the most surprising concerned the GWR's 1947 decision to commission 200 0-6-0 pannier tanks of '4F' power class. These were to a new design and were intended for heavy shunting and were numbered 8400-99 and 9400-99. Table 1 (see p35), which delineates the pre-nationalisation classes built, reveals that these tank engines continued to keep Swindon Works, the former GWR's hallowed centre of mechanical engineering for a century, occupied until 1956.

As can be seen from Table 2 (see p36), Riddles and his team produced a comprehensive range of new Standards. The first to appear was the '7P6F' (later 7MT) 'Britannia' class of Pacifics, which debuted from Crewe Works in January 1951. This type, and the '9F' 2-10-0 freight design, were generally well received and the latter can lay a claim to being the most outstanding locomotive ever built in the UK.

Reviewing Riddles' policy, there is no doubt that parts of BR's steam fleet was in need of replacement and this process was in arrears, mainly due to the war. The time was not right for extensive introduction of diesel traction because of inadequate experience in the UK, though railcars had already proved themselves and their use could have been expanded. Riddles sent no fact-finding delegation to examine developments in North America with diesel power and these decisions, coupled with the ignoring of the Harrington Committee proposal in 1951 for a large-scale main line diesel trial, make it hard not to conclude he was against this form of traction.

It must not be forgotten, though, that a main line diesel of equivalent power to steam costs over twice the price and Chapter 1 has made it plain that the BTC did not have the money for an extensive trial with this form of traction.

Staging the Interchange Trials taught nothing that could not have been determined more cheaply by other means. Further, the '8P' power type selected for the trials was not one that was required going forward. Designing 12 new Standard types was wasteful when the small numbers of some classes is borne in mind.

Sufficient evidence already existed to expand the use of diesel railcars, as opposed to constructing small, low-powered steam engines at higher cost. Ordering 200 heavy shunting tank engines for the WR seems to owe more to keeping Swindon busy than the more rational solution, taken by the LMSR in the 1930s, to opt instead for an equivalent diesel shunter.

There is no doubt that the 'Britannia' class of Pacifics and 2-10-0 '9Fs' were needed and did much good work. It was sensible to continue to build pre-nationalisation types for specific situations and, in fact, their total number exceeded the Riddles Standards by 50%. Whether it was necessary to replace 10% of the inherited fleet with more steam is highly questionable. For sure, there was no real operating reason to construct the prototype '8P' Pacific, No 71000, just because LMSR '8P' No 46202 had been written off in a serious accident. The exercise can be judged to be largely an ego trip for Riddles, Cox and his design team.

What is mystifying is how this farce came about. Missenden, the RE chairman, had been the Southern Railway General Manager and Riddles was but one of a cabinet of Members of the Executive. Perhaps part of the answer lies in Missenden permitting the Southern's CME, Bulleid, free rein so Riddles benefited from what had been the norm before nationalisation.

Bonavia perhaps gives a clue to the dynamics within the Executive by saying that Missenden's successor attempted to build bridges with the BTC and address frustrations at Chief Regional Officer level. He, however, concludes these attempts by the new RE chairman came too late and the organisation, and Riddles, involvement in BR, ended in 1953.

A parting bouquet must be handed to Riddles for his work towards standardisation of methods and equipment within his domain, which saw the number of steam classes reduced under his leadership from 448 to 293. Sadly, no such progress was made by the Operating Department. No attempt was made to look at a national pattern of passenger services that ignored the boundaries of the former Big Four pre-nationalisation railways. Thus many trains along the former Midland route between Birmingham and Bristol terminated there, rather than continuing forward to the West Country. Rationalisation of routes, notably in the East Midlands coalfield, cried out for action and the laying-in of short spurs to connect parallel tracks of pre-nationalisation competitors but nothing was done and a great opportunity to solve a problem that was to bite the railways hard in the early 1960s was lost. The BTC had been set up to co-ordinate transport, yet it made no effort towards this, whilst on the railways the RE's Operating Department did very little to better co-ordinate operations.

Was Riddles right?

Riddles' decision to continue to build steam locomotives and to effectively ignore main line diesel traction is one of the most controversial aspects of BR's history. Perhaps it is timely to assess the issues involved.

The main constraint under which Riddles was operating was a lack of capital. This meant electrification on a large scale was ruled out. A second constraint was a shortage of petroleum products, which were rationed, and he would have seen the debacle of the Government's scheme for the conversion of steam locomotives to burn oil. Introducing a large number of diesels would have most probably been met with inadequate fuel to run them. Finally, diesels cost significantly more to build than does steam, so you can have more of the latter for the same price as the former.

A factor that has never been mentioned in this debate is the potential of diesel traction in 1948. North American locomotive builders were no more advanced than EE in this country and the most powerful single-unit locomotive of a size capable of being used in the UK was the LMSR prototype No 10000. This was rated at 1,600hp and so could be regarded as equal to a Class 5 steam engine driven flat out or a Class 6 in normal traffic (3,000 pounds of coal per hour, the BR standard firing rate).

Nos 10000/1 were experimental and EE learned a lot from their operation but the capital cost of a fleet of the type, running them in multiple as an alternative to a single steam engine, was a non-starter. It would therefore have been very unwise to have saddled BR with a large number of locomotives of this type and whose train heating equipment was so unreliable as to cause them to be confined to freight work during the winter!

Diesel technology moved quite quickly and the rating of No 10203 at 2,000hp in 1954 also represented the highest power available for a British application. Even then, the ER judged this to be inadequate for East Coast expresses.

Continuing to build steam, however modern in design, failed to address three issues. First, cities were becoming fed up with the pollution associated with its operation. Secondly, steam was labour-intensive at a time of full employment when men could get better paid and cleaner jobs elsewhere and the railways were habitually short of staff. Thirdly, whilst oil was in short supply, so was locomotive coal.

Should Riddles have built any new steam locomotives at all? Ironically, the LNER was the least profitable of the Big Four but had the best provision of Classes 7 and 8 traction but these types are only part of a fleet. Riddles had no way of knowing when funds for significant miles of electrification would be forthcoming and it seems fair to say that renewal of the main line fleet was needed in quite a few areas. Proof of this is that steam continued to be ordered long after he had retired.

It is fair to conclude he had no option for long-distance passenger and freight services. Conversely, he should have been more open-minded about the benefits of diesel for secondary passenger and branch lines, based on the highly-successful GWR railcars and the significant cost and labour savings.

As a postscript, in 1951 the Ministry of Fuel & Power entered into a consultation across Whitehall on national fuel policy. The steam versus modern traction issue was the topic for a discussion paper produced by the MoT.

Advantages for diesel power were given as higher annual mileages and better acceleration which offered the potential for more services on busy routes, counterbalanced by higher capital costs. Diesel locomotives were judged to need less examination and maintenance than steam but there was the potential of a risk to fuel supply from overseas during a 'national emergency', a euphemism presumably for a war, just six years after the end of the last one.

Construction costs were given as £16,000 for main line steam and £78,000 for a comparable diesel. Coal consumption was 48 pounds per mile and 1.4 gallons of diesel respectively but it was doubted whether the greater thermal efficiency of the diesel could outweigh the significantly-higher cost of its fuel. A breakeven cost of fuel was put at 1s 3d (6p) per mile.

Turning to shunting motive power, construction costs were £5,800 for steam and £19,600 for diesel. Fuel consumption per hour was 233 pounds of coal and 2.5 gallons of oil respectively. By virtue of fuel not being required by the diesel during periods of inactivity, the diesel shunter cost 2s 3d (11p) as against 6s (30p) worth of coal per hour. These figures show why the LMSR had decided to only build diesels for shunting.

The document states that there was no plan to increase the number of main line diesels beyond the five built or on order until more information on costs, particularly operating and maintenance, was available. The case for diesel power in yards which operated on either a two- or three-shift basis was now accepted.

Electric traction was viewed as having the same advantages as diesel and it was acknowledged that it used less coal per mile than steam where power was generated in coal-fired power stations. Electrification was predicted on any passenger route to lead to a significant rise in demand and so more services.

Perversely, the report argues that this causes an increase in total coal required and so starts to wipe out the lower absolute tonnage of coal. This was relevant when trying to ascertain how much coal needed to be produced.

The obvious disadvantage of electrification was the capital cost. In the report on electrification produced in 1950, the BTC had calculated that a minimum traffic density of between 3 and 4 million trailing ton miles per mile of single track was required to justify electrification and that 30% of the network carried this density in 1949. The report concludes that the RE had identified a number of electrification schemes but constraints on capital, materials and manpower were delaying progress.

Table 1 Pre-nationalisation types built after nationalisation

	1948	1949	1950	1951	1952	1953	1954	1955	1956	Total
GWR										
4-6-0 Castle	10	10	10	-	-	-	-	-	-	*30*
4-6-0 Hall	15	11	23	-	-	-	-	-	-	*49*
4-6-0 Manor	-	-	10	-	-	-	-	-	-	*10*
0-6-0 2251	2	-	-	-	-	-	-	-	-	*2*
2-6-2T 5101	10	10	-	-	-	-	-	-	-	*20*
0-6-0T 15XX	-	10	-	-	-	-	-	-	-	*10*
0-6-0T 16XX	-	20	10	20	-	-	5	15	-	*70*
0-6-0T 57XX	11	10		-	-	-	-	-	-	*21*
0-6-0T 67XX	6	4	10	-	-	-	-	-	-	*20*
0-6-0T 74XX	10	-	10	-	-	-	-	-	-	*20*
0-6-0ST 94XX	-	13	53	43	50	11	18	3	9	*200*
LMS										
4-6-2 Class 8	1	-	-	-	-	-	-	-	-	*1*
4-6-0 Class 5	40	32	26	2	-	-	-	-	-	*100*
2-6-0 Class 4	20	27	47	58	7	-	-	-	-	*159*
2-6-0 Class 2	15	-	30	30	20	13	-	-	-	*108*
2-6-4T Class 4	46	30	54	17	-	-	-	-	-	*147*
2-6-2T Class 2	20	30	30	10	30	-	-	-	-	*120*
0-4-0 Dock	-	-	-	-	-	4	1	-	-	*5*
LNER										
4-6-2 A1	21	28	-	-	-	-	-	-	-	*49*
4-6-2 A2	14	-	-	-	-	-	-	-	-	*14*
4-6-0 B1	68	18	24	19	7	-	-	-	-	*136*
2-6-0 K1	-	61	9	-	-	-	-	-	-	*70*
2-6-4T L1	59	15	25	-	-	-	-	-	-	*99*
0-6-0T J72	-	15	5	8	-	-	-	-	-	*28*
SR										
4-6-2 Merchant Navy	8	2	-	-	-	-	-	-	-	*10*
4-6-2 West Country	19	11	9	1	-	-	-	-	-	*40*

Totals: GWR=452, LMS=640, LNER=396, SR=50; combined=1,538

Table 2 BR Standard designs

	1951	1952	1953	1954	1955	1956	1957	1958	1959	1960	Total
4-6-2 Class 8	-	-	-	1	-	-	-	-	-	-	1
4-6-2 Class 7	25	13	7	10	-	-	-	-	-	-	55
4-6-2- Class 6	2	8	-	-	-	-	-	-	-	-	10
4-6-0 Class 5	29	1	20	25	44	30	23	-	-	-	172
4-6-0 Class 4	16	4	25	5	13	5	12	-	-	-	80
2-6-0 Class 4	-	10	25	10	15	19	36	-	-	-	115
2-6-0 Class 3	-	-	-	20	-	-	-	-	-	-	20
2-6-0 Class 2	-	4	8	33	10	10	-	-	-	-	65
2-6-4T Class 4	17	37	18	36	23	20	4	-	-	-	155
2-6-2T Class 3	-	20	-	12	13	-	-	-	-	-	45
2-6-2T Class 2	-	-	20	-	-	-	10	-	-	-	30
2-10-0 Class 9	-	-	-	32	38	45	56	62	15	3	251
Total	89	97	123	184	156	129	141	62	15	3	999

Chapter 3

Modernising British Railways

This chapter takes the story through the first stages of modernisation to the point where detailed proposals had been drawn up as a basis for the 1955 Modernisation Plan. The Plan itself and public reaction to it follow in the next chapter.

A lightweight diversion
Passing reference was made in the previous chapter to the setting up by the RE in 1951 of a Lightweight Trains Committee (LTC) under the chairmanship of H. G. Bowles, the Assistant CRO of the WR. The remit of the committee was to come up with proposals for a low-cost solution for branch line passenger trains with a view to making these services viable. Once identified, the Committee was to propose areas where trials could be conducted.

Between 1950 and 1953 Ireland witnessed the arrival of 80 railcars based on the GWR format, 20 in Ulster and the remainder in the south. As part of the information gathering, the Committee visited the island and was accompanied by Frank Pope, who had recently become a Commission Member after vacating the post of chairman of the Ulster Transport Authority. Visits were also made to the Continent and a first report was produced in March 1952. Diesel railcars were judged to be the best option on the grounds of lowest cost, best availability and fastest schedules. A diesel-mechanical drivetrain was recommended for powers up to 500hp, which reflected that used in the AEC vehicles built for the GWR and Ireland.

Bearing in mind Riddles' views on steam versus diesel explained in Chapter 2, the steam lobby within the RE counter-proposed a push-pull trainset powered by BR Standard Class 2 2-6-2Ts. When the costs for these were calculated to be nearly twice that of a diesel railcar, it was clear what the Commission would decide.

Trials were proposed in Lincolnshire, the West Riding and the western half of Cumberland. Fear that new railcars would be viewed by the Lincolnshire bus operator (also part of the BTC) as too competitive meant that this area was shelved but then reinstated. Authority was given for eight sets for the West Riding and 13 each for Cumberland, East Anglia and Lincolnshire.

In September 1952 the Carriage & Wagon Drawing Office at Derby initiated an investigation into a new design of railcar. It was decided that construction would be in heavy-duty light alloy in order to give the power-to-weight ratio necessary for the services envisaged and also employing integral body and underframe construction; the standard LMSR suburban coach length of 57ft was adopted. ICI Metals Division was invited to cooperate in the choice of materials for this body structure.

Following a competitive tender, the Leyland L600 six-cylinder diesel engine of 125bhp was chosen, with two engines per vehicle and, in view of the steeply-graded routes on which the units were to be used, both cars in the set were to be powered. Whereas the LTC had recommended a diesel-mechanical drive, Riddles wanted to use the Leyland Lysholm-Smith TRC 5/2 torque converter and Walker Bros final drive. This transmission had been fitted in the LMSR railcar of 1938, with which Riddles was familiar. Unfortunately, by then Leyland had superseded the torque converter for road transport applications and no further development had been carried out on, what was now, an obsolete piece of equipment. Some might say that this continued choice of obsolete equipment mirrored Riddles' dogged attachment to steam traction!

West Riding travellers between Leeds, Bradford and Harrogate were the first to see the new designs and the new service commenced on 14 June 1954. A diesel maintenance facility was built at the ex-Great Northern Railway steam shed at Bradford Hammerton Street, which continued to service steam until 1958.

Whilst construction of the West Riding sets was in progress, Derby Works undertook a redesign of the powertrain, possibly prompted by Riddles' retirement. The two leading diesel engine manufacturers, Leyland and AEC, began a joint venture known as British United Traction (BUT) to supply power equipment to the rail industry and the engine type chosen for all subsequent lightweight railcars was a BUT six-cylinder model rated at 150bhp. Out went Riddles' favoured Leyland Lysholm-Smith torque converter in favour of a fluid coupling and mechanical drive through a four-speed epicyclic gearbox. This drivetrain became the standard for the majority of railcars ordered over the following five years.

West Cumberland was the next area to be dealt with. By virtue of the less-demanding gradients, only one vehicle in the two-car set was powered. 'Derby Lightweight' sets were built for Lincolnshire, East Anglia, Tyne and Wearside, East Manchester, North Wales and Birmingham in two- and four-car formations, with deliveries continuing into the second half of 1956.

Finally Derby built two cars with cabs at both ends to enable operation as single cars for very lightly-used services and these went from new to ply between Bletchley, Buckingham and Banbury. A battery-powered electric version appeared in 1958 for trials on the Ballater branch from Aberdeen.

Meanwhile, a tender to the rail industry in 1954 resulted in a winning bid by Metro-Cammell. It is worth reporting the minutes of the Commission's meeting on 29 April when the order was approved that, in view of the large sum involved, attempts should be made to negotiate a lower price. This was an attitude that was to recur repeatedly where contracts with the private sector builders were concerned.

Although these employed the standard BUT powertrain, construction was from steel, not light alloy, and this saved money to the detriment of an extra five tons in weight. These sets were a precursor to the type of construction employed in the squadron production Modernisation Plan DMUs and they were delivered to north Manchester and East Anglia during 1955.

Derby's design proved far from durable in everyday service. Front-end crush damage could occur during heavy shunting, whilst a car could sag and the doors jam shut when carrying a heavy passenger load! Being able to couple in multiple was useful during times of peak demand. The problem was, however, that the West Riding batch had a 'Red Triangle' coupling code whereas the remaining Derbys and the Met-Cams were 'Yellow Diamond'. Both of these were incompatible with the subsequent standard for DMUs with a mechanical transmission, which was 'Blue Square'.

These lightweight sets had a very positive impact on train loadings and the Bletchley to Banbury line is claimed to have seen a growth of 43% in patronage. Nevertheless, the rise in revenue and reduction in costs was insufficient in many cases to turn a loss-making branch into a profitable one and closures meant DMUs of all types began to become surplus during the 1960s. Being non-standard and (in the case of the Derby sets) suffering structural issues, the obvious choice for eliminating the rolling stock surplus was the withdrawal of these pioneers.

Inter-city DMU inauguration

In 1951 the Inglis Report had reviewed transport in Glasgow. Among its recommendations was the elimination of steam by the substitution of electrification on services along the Queen Street Low Level corridor, primarily those to Helensburgh and Airdrie. Nothing was done to progress the proposals for rail and it is also worth noting that Inglis recommended ripping up the tram network. Part of the problem confronting the Commission was a lack of capital and it tried over quite a period to persuade the city council to collaborate on funding.

Meanwhile, Edinburgh City Council was bleating to the BTC about locomotive smoke pollution emanating from Waverley station. Riddles' Standard steam classes were of no benefit in this respect!

On 29 April 1953 the Commission's Chief Secretary submitted a memo recommending the Railway Executive be asked to try to progress the Inglis recommendations and that those relating to the introduction of diesel services between Glasgow and Edinburgh should be implemented as soon as possible on the basis put forward by the Lightweight Trains Committee. These were stopping services and included those from Central and Buchanan Street as well as those from Queen Street.

Contractors (the word used by the BTC and British Railways to denote private sector manufacturers) were to be invited to bid for the contract to build the required DMUs. In addition, the RE was to come up with a proposal for the substitution of DMUs on some of the regular local fast steam services between Edinburgh Waverley and Glasgow Queen Street.

The Inglis Report was becoming a political hot potato now and the Commission discussed the matter again on 28 May because of interest in the Report by the Minister of Transport and the Secretary of State for Scotland. At the meeting of the Works Committee on 15 October it was agreed that a recommendation be put to the Commission for four eight-car DMUs (six power cars per set) to cover 13 trains per day each way (replicating the prevailing service) and with one spare set. For the Central to Princes Street route, two trainsets of three cars (all powered) was recommended for five return trips, the high power-to-weight ratio being required because of the steep climb up the lower Clyde valley. The BTC approved these proposals on 29 October.

As was to prove to be the case time and again over the next decade, finger-in-the-wind estimates of modernisation requirements proved to be wide of the mark, as a memo of 16 September 1954 to the Commission demonstrates. The original scheme had envisaged a requirement for 36 power cars and 10 trailers but a detailed examination then revised this to 31 power cars and 15 trailers, which included spare vehicles.

By the time of the above memo, the WR was reviewing options for its Birmingham Snow Hill to Cardiff and Swansea route. As noted in the previous chapter, the GWR had introduced a premium service between these cities in 1934 using a single railcar for which a supplementary fare was payable. By now, these railcars were past their prime for such a service and the WR stated it wanted to augment the prevailing steam-powered trains with two daily return journeys using new lightweight diesel trains, the terminology used in the official papers.

The WR admitted that a detail proposal had yet to be worked out, but the new service was expected to generate substantial additional traffic. This was because of 'major extension' planned by the Steel Company of Wales during the next three or four years and the relationship these developments would have with the engineering interests in the Midlands. Journey time savings of 30 minutes to Cardiff and 60 minutes overall to Swansea were envisaged. It was anticipated that six three-car sets, requiring 12 power cars and six trailers, would be required.

Swindon Works was given responsibility for the project and a common form for both these inter-city trains had been agreed and design work was already in progress by the date of the memo of 16 September. This was seeking Commission approval to order powertrains (two per vehicle) and control gear from BUT for a total of 43 power cars and 21 trailers. The argument for the advance order for the WR sets was that any over-ordering of BUT's standard 150hp powertrains could be absorbed in future schemes. BTC authority came eventually on 12 May 1955.

By virtue of the control system adopted, a non-standard unit coupling code, 'White Circle', was needed, which ruled out connection to other DMUs. A vehicle length of 64ft 6in, was longer than the Derby's Lightweights and, although described as lightweight trains, Swindon substituted steel for alloy, which pushed the weight up and the power-to-weight ratio down.

The final configuration became a three-car set, made up of two power cars and one trailer. Uniquely, one driving cab was full-width, whilst the other had a centre gangway to permit two sets to couple and create a six-car formation with access throughout. For three-car sets, there ended up five vehicle types to meet ScR and WR requirements! Such a lack of standardisation – only three types of vehicle were truly needed – pushed up costs but Regional Managers didn't worry about that. Both the full- and half-width front ends suffered from unimaginative styling. Top speed was 70mph, the norm for all diesel-mechanical multiple units.

Delivery of the 64 vehicles for both schemes was scheduled from December 1955 to August 1956 and August to December 1956 respectively. Although the Minister of Transport viewed a completed set in 1956, public viewing in Scotland was not until 4 January 1957 with a partial timetable inaugurated on the 7th.

Contemporary reports about the Scottish inauguration refer to insufficient sets being available and a shortage of diesel fuel. The timing was 60 minutes for 47 miles, including one stop. Delivery of the WR's sets followed later, with two (typically) six-car formations each making just one daily return journey. In hindsight, this first stab at an inter-city train by BR offered very little beyond a basic DMU. Under BR's motive power classification, the sets became Class 126. Swindon modified aspects of the design during the building of, what were dubbed, the 'Cross Country' trains (later Class 120) and these had the standard DMU 'Blue Square' coupling code.

A development programme for BR

Chapters 1 and 2 have provided the background for the state of British Railways in 1953. Starved of funds for capital projects since nationalisation, it had been difficult to finance the repair of war damage and the arrears of maintenance that had accrued since 1939. The RE had pursued a policy of motive power development that was largely focused on the steam locomotive, even though it stood alone among national railways in this and did not enjoy BTC support in so doing. Belatedly, it had begun to look at diesel railcars as a way forward for rural lines and suburban services.

Of course railway modernisation covers more than motive power and some post-nationalisation projects were referred to in Chapter 1. Commission Member Reginald Wilson, who had contacts in the MoT and the Treasury, encouraged the BTC at the time of the October 1951 election to put down on paper railway capital requirements. Subsequently he encouraged the RE to draw up a long-term plan for its capital needs. Wilson was supported by fellow Commission Members Pope and Barker, who agreed that the Government could be receptive to modernisation proposals.

A committee of five senior RE officers, again chaired by Harrington (who had chaired the committee on forms of motive power referred to in the previous chapter) and including John Ratter and S. B. Warder (the RE's Chief Civil and Electrical Engineers), was set up in 1952 to prepare a paper indicating 10 salient directions in which additional capital might be expended, on the assumption that Treasury approval might be given to a global additional investment authorisation of perhaps £500 million spent over the next 10-20 years. The amount sought is interesting because Sir John Elliot, by then the RE Chairman, quoted an initial figure of £100 million.

The committee produced 'A Development Programme for British Railways' in April 1953 and this was considered at the RE's meeting on the 30th. Its opening paragraph states:

'The British Railways system is a great national asset; the railways form the country's largest industrial trading undertaking and provide a public service vital for the life of the nation.'

It continued by referring to the railways forming the 'backbone' for transportation of coal, raw materials for the iron and steel industries and high-density short-distance passenger traffic. Despite the growth of road transport, it argued that the railways could not be allowed to run down due to a lack of investment for modernisation. Reference was made to the goal of implementing modern methods of operation based on technical progress and this is an issue that will be referred to later.

Postwar severe limits on capital for investment and shortages of steel, non-ferrous metals and labour were brought up, as was the fact that significant scientific, technical and engineering advancements had taken place but BR had been unable to benefit from these. Important studies had been initiated into the rationalisation of traffic flows and the reorganisation of working methods, though it is unclear now just what these were. What was now sought was 'the ability to take advantage of the immense possibilities now opened up to reap the harvest of a rich reward in considerable advances in efficiency, in greatly improved standards of service and in substantial economies in working is dependent on the injection of new capital on a substantial scale to allow of the construction of the requisite facilities and the introduction of the new equipment and materials'. Very high-minded, and verbose!

Its proposals were to be additional to the normal programme of capital renewal and comprised for each of ten areas the minimum essential investment; when combined the total cost was exactly £500 million.

Table 3 1953 Development programme for BR

Proposals	Estimated cost £m
Electrification	160
Major improvements to running lines	60
Modernisation of signalling and telecoms	30
Re-siting and modernisation of marshalling yards	50
Rationalisation and modernisation of freight terminals	50
Fitting of continuous brake to freight rolling stock	40
Introduction of diesel railcars	17
Reconstruction of passenger stations	40
Helicopter terminals and services	40
Marine services	13
Total	500

It is clear from Table 3 that there was no role for main line diesel locomotives, whereas electrification was to encompass all the main routes out of London. The paper went to the Commission in May but this coincided with passage of the 1953 Transport Act and the BTC was preoccupied with the outwash from that legislation. In the circumstances, the RE viewed the paper as a blueprint which the post-October 1953 BTC might take forward.

Formulation of the 1955 Modernisation Plan

It would be an unfortunate metaphor to say that a head of steam had built up for modernisation by 1954. A WR management meeting on 27 January reported that the Regional Manager had directed that a Committee had been appointed to report generally on the development of diesel services in the WR, comprising nominated representatives of the Operating, Commercial and Motive Power Departments, with additional assistance from certain technical officers. The Birmingham area was to be dealt with as a first stage in the Committee's negotiations.

Even though Sir Brian Robertson was still setting up a headquarters hierarchy for the Commission, plans for railway modernisation were, effectively, launched at the BTC's meeting on 14 April 1954. This followed discussions in February with Whitehall Departments. On the 10th the Chancellor of the Exchequer said he was 'ready to consider proposals for helping railways, but opposed to any form of Government subsidy'. Meanwhile the Ministry of Fuel & Power continued to press the MoT for railway plans for the extension of electrification, a topic referred to in Chapter 2.

As has been seen already, the first programme for the introduction of modern railcars was under way, whilst the Commission had sanctioned the purchase of 170 sets of equipment for 350hp diesel shunters from English Electric at its meeting on 11 February 1954, with construction to be undertaken in BR's workshops during 1955 and 1956.

Sir Daril Watson, the Chief of General Services, was instructed to assemble a Planning Committee, which he would chair, composed of Chief Officers and representatives from the Regions, the members being:

David Blee (Chief of Commercial Services)
Michael Bonavia (Chief Officer, New Works)
R. C. Bond (Chief Officer, Mechanical Engineering)
J. L. Harrington (Chief Officer, Marine and Administration)
E. S. Hunt (Assistant Regional Manager, LMR)

C. C. Inglis (Chief Research Officer)
S. E. Parkhouse (Chief of Operating Services)
A. J. Pearson (Chief Administrative Officer)
H. H. Phillips (Assistant Regional Manager, WR)
V. Radford (Chief of Budgets)
J. Ratter (Chief Officer, Civil Engineering)
A. E. Robson (Chief Officer, Carriage & Wagon Engineering)
S. B. Warder (Chief Officer, Electrical Engineering)
Messrs Harvey (Chief Officer Motive Power) and Pickford (Commercial Superintendent, WR) joined later.

The Planning Committee was to submit proposals to the BTC for modernisation, making the following assumptions:

- The Plan shall be spread over a period of years; in principle the Plan is capable of being launched within five years and completed within 15.
- That Her Majesty's Government will provide a loan of the order of £500 million on special terms.

Note there was no intention of securing a grant but instead a loan, repayable with interest, out of the extra surplus derived from modernisation. As a basis, the Committee was to first submit a brief analysis of the traffics on which they considered the Plan should be based, and traffic forecasts for all significant aspects of passenger and freight business to 1970 were compiled. The Committee was to make early recommendations to the BTC regarding any action which they thought was desirable for strengthening the technical staff necessary to prepare and execute the Plan.

The eventual recommendation of the Committee was to be the inclusion of proposals for priorities to be awarded to various elements in the Plan. The Committee would have the power to co-opt specialist officers for assistance on special subjects. Regional Managers were to be consulted and the Committee was to report to the BTC from time to time when it required any further directions.

Watson set up nine sub-committees covering the following subjects: Forecast & brief analysis of traffic; Forms of Motive Power; Modernisation of passenger & goods stations; Modernisation of carriage & wagon stocks; Modernisation & resiting of marshalling yards; Continuous braking of freight stock; Way & works, Signalling & Telecommunications; Build-up of technical staff; ships & packet ports. Taking the Forms of Motive Power sub-committee by way of example, its membership comprised Phillips (chairman), Bonavia (Chief Officer New Works), Bond, Harvey (Chief Officer, Motive Power), Pickford (Commercial Superintendent, WR) and Warder plus four others.

The mechanical engineering representatives on the Committee had to admit, with some embarrassment, that they had shown no interest in the prototype main line diesels and were unable to provide accurate figures that would help. They felt a conservative break-even of 70,000 miles per annum should be used. This, of course, helped their case for retaining a steam-based motive power policy.

Whilst 40,000 miles per annum might be a fair overall average for a steam locomotive of Class 7 and above, it was definitely very low for a comparable diesel, where a figure of 70,000 would be expected. In 1952 only some 400 steam locomotives achieved this.

A report on the performance of the existing main line diesels was prepared instead by the SR, which had been using all six diesel-electrics for a couple of years, and it was favourable. A second report compared capital and running costs for a Class 7 steam engine as against a 2,000hp diesel and concluded that the advantage lay with the diesel for annual mileages over 40,000.

Bonavia has given an insight into the discussions within the Forms of Motive Power Sub-Committee. The electrification lobby's case was hampered by the economists' refusal to agree that the 'sparks effect' would apply to main lines in the way that suburban schemes had seen tremendous growth in passenger volumes. This cast doubt on the economics of main line schemes and persuaded some to favour diesel instead. Schemes based on the latter could be implemented more quickly and cheaply and also offered greater flexibility in that diesel locomotives could be redeployed if a decision was taken later to opt for electrification.

The diesel lobby struggled because of the amount of hard data about the existing prototypes and the inexperience of British manufacturers in main line diesel production. In hindsight, it is strange that the only visit to North America to study how the transition to diesel had been accomplished over the previous 20 years was made by S. B. Warder in 1954.

Finally, the steam lobby argued that first-cost was considerably cheaper than for modern traction and they cited instances of high availability and high-speed performances achieved in specific instances by steam. This meant this form of traction could achieve everything required in terms of timetable improvements.

Whilst there was truth in the above case for steam, the performances referred to were either one-offs or used hand-picked locomotives. For example, the choice of locomotives for the summer 'Elizabethan' London to Edinburgh non-stop service was made the previous year and the selected traction was put through Doncaster Works for overhaul in advance. The BR firing limit of 3,000 pounds of coal per hour imposed a ceiling on long, sustained high-power running by steam. Part of the success of the BR Standard Class 7MT 'Britannias' in East Anglia was that the London to Norwich journey lasted two hours, meaning footplate crews got a respite. Such duration was short by standards prevailing on the West Coast lines and the London to Plymouth route.

So it was that the prospects of better acceleration and hill-climbing at the turn of a handle, greater overall availability and reliability and cleanliness as key elements in a bid to win more traffic decided the sub-committee to come down in favour of modern traction.

Based on the above thinking, on 4 June the Regions came up with the following views on the implementation of dieselisation:

WR – Eliminate all steam working west of Newton Abbot and use diesel units based in that area for hauling a large proportion of the passenger and freight traffic from the West to London and Bristol. A preliminary examination considered that 105 main line diesels could displace 191 steam. This proposal differed from the original intention noted above to focus initially on the Birmingham area, probably because it confined the trial to a defined area.

SR – Greatest advantage would probably be secured by employing about 100 of the heaviest locomotives to replace 129 steam between Waterloo and Exeter/Southampton, Bournemouth and Weymouth. 'Considerable time' needed to work on proposal.

LMR – Dieselisation of Devons Road (East London), with 26 trip and seven shunting locomotives replacing 41 steam.

NER – Bradford 'most promising' area but no detailed plan; based on timetable changes, suggested about 40 locomotives could be used.

ER – Several possibilities for experimenting with diesel but scope appears to be limited. Regional Manager considered Region's problems can best be solved by electrification. Region in discussion with NER and ScR because 2,000hp locomotives not considered adequate for prevailing ECML schedules, let alone improvements, and have in mind a power of 3,000hp.

ScR – No zones suitable for dieselisation. Basically, the Regional Manager wanted electrification, especially suburban. Floated idea of basing diesels at

Newcastle for use north thereof to replace steam Pacifics and possibly other types.

On 17 August the Planning Committee reported to the Commission that its deliberations had now reached the final stage. The nine sub-committees, composed of both HQ and regional officers, had been considering the different aspects of motive power. It was clear that substantial changeover from steam would be recommended on grounds of economy alone, and thus proved the case for diesel traction. The issue for debate lay in the ultimate balance of the advantage between diesel working and electrification on main line services.

Watson noted that steps were being taken to deal with the need associated with more technically-advanced equipment for a large increase in technical staff who could advise. Bearing in mind his army background, he wondered whether the Royal Engineers might be able to assist.

Two days later, the Commission considered Watson's memo, together with submissions from the ScR Regional Manager and from the regional Committee on the electrification of the Glasgow suburban lines. The issue with the latter was that a forecast rise of 50% in patronage after electrification would still result in net costs rising. Watson had floated the idea of treating the project as a special case, where social impact outweighed viability. He did, though, say DMUs were to be considered as an alternative. In the view of the Commission Members:

- The BTC do not expect the Plan will cover the electrification of the majority of their main lines, since money, time and staff will not be available to deal with the electrification of more than those lines that carry traffic of a certain density.
- If the Planning Committee gives reasonable justification on the basis of the reports dealing with the performance of the diesels, which the BTC already possesses, and any other reports it has got, it will look sympathetically at a proposal for a bold programme for the trial of diesel locomotives.

Meanwhile, mindful that the volume of work to be undertaken would exceed the capacity of its own workshops, on 27 May the Commission considered the implications of this situation and the minutes record the following decision. The Chairman referred to offers of discussions with manufacturing representatives regarding the construction of locomotives in future years, and the need for formulating the policy regarding manufacturing in BTC's works.

After members of the BTC expressed their views, Mr Train was requested to give a synopsis of the suggested line to be adopted when meeting manufacturers, and to submit proposals for the manner in which a review of BTC's manufacturing objectives and facilities for the construction of locomotives and rolling stock should be undertaken.

Train produced a memo dated 14 October covering (a) a request from the Locomotive Manufacturers Association for a meeting to discuss the placing of orders for locomotives with its members and (b) the suggested review of the BTC's manufacturing objectives and facilities for the construction of locomotives and rolling stock. It was agreed that the BTC did not wish to meet the LMA until after a joint report on the comparative costs of locomotive building by railways and by contractors had been received and studied. It was also agreed that it was not necessary to take definitive action in connection with this review, since the Modernisation Plan, which would have a major bearing on this matter, would soon be considered.

This all might sound very cumbersome but two factors need to be borne in mind. Public procurement where values are significant needs to be handled transparently to avoid any whiff of corruption. Secondly, the BTC was always scared stiff of the railway unions, a view based on much reading of Commission minutes. Any move to use contractors was seen by the rail unions as work that could potentially be done by their members in railway shops.

Armed with the Commission's views from the 19 August meeting, Watson's team and the Regional Managers met on 9 September and discussed Regional proposals for main line diesels. It was agreed that the WR should submit a detailed plan for all-diesel working in a selected area and that the other Regions should consider similar arrangements. There was some debate on the choice between competing types of traction and this will be covered in the chapter on the so-called Pilot Scheme.

The Planning Committee submitted a 43-page report in October and this put forward 12 proposals costed at £1.17million. Some of the key elements bear consideration here.

The Committee foresaw a long-term and growing need for the railways to be the principal haulier of coal and minerals, together with a similar growth in demand for general merchandise shipments. Concerning passenger traffic forecasts, the report noted the decline in short-distance patronage outside the main industrial areas and this traffic was described as uneconomic. It was envisaged that the railways would withdraw from this business in due course.

A growth in living standards was expected and this had, over the previous 30 years, seen a consequential rise in travel. Some of this demand was forecast to be met by road and air competitors but the railways could look forward to extra revenue too. Interestingly, there was no mention of expanded car ownership and therefore the impact this would have on train travel.

On Way & Works, the report had looked at permanent speed restrictions in key locations and evaluated the benefits in time saving when set against the cost of elimination. A target maximum speed of 90mph (not 100mph) was proposed for main lines wherever possible.

Colour-light signalling, power signalboxes and centralised train control were to increase operating efficiency, whilst the installation of automatic train control (later renamed automatic warning system [aws]) was aimed at improving safety.

There was recognition that telecommunications was a key component in running a modern railway and there was a need for upgrading.

A further proposal related to motive power and envisaged the progressive replacement of steam by electric and diesel traction. Surprisingly, the construction of steam locomotives was to continue for 'a few years'. Steam was said not to offer the required standards of acceleration and cleanliness for a modern railway. Nevertheless, by 1970 7,130 steam engines were planned to still be in traffic. The change in traction provision was forecast as shown in Table 4:

Table 4 Motive power transition to 1970

	Existing or authorised	1970
Steam locomotives	18,337	7,139
Electric locomotives	71	471
EMU vehicles	4,805	7,286
Diesel main line locomotives	9	3,669
Diesel shunting locomotives	770	1,970
DMU vehicles	277	5,726

Over 900 miles of routes were put forward for electrification and encompassed:

- London, Tilbury & Southend.
- Liverpool Street to Enfield and Chingford, extension to Hertford and Bishop's Stortford.
- King's Cross and Moorgate to Hitchin and Letchworth (including Hertford Loop).
- Glasgow suburban (subject to agreement being reached with Glasgow Corporation as regards local transport).
- Remaining main lines of SR Eastern and Central Divisions (London to

Ramsgate, Dover and Folkestone having been sanctioned already).
- ECML to Leeds and possibly York.

These proposals were chosen because they linked in with existing or authorised schemes.

Dieselisation was to be implemented in discrete areas and steam depots closed, with every effort to be made to eliminate mixed steam and diesel working in a selected area. The LMR planned on displacing 1,200 steam with 930 diesel locomotives on services between Euston, Birmingham, Liverpool and Manchester. These numbers seem now to reflect the inexperience of Committee members in modern traction. WR plans for the West Country and SR plans to displace steam in Wessex have already been referred to.

Locomotives for use on heavy freight work were envisaged as needing modification to cope with the task. What seems astonishing now is that the engineers on the Committee believed this would entail additional cost and it is hard to understand their thinking here!

There was disappointment that the existing diesels had not achieved a high enough level of utilisation to support an economic case for replacing steam but the Committee was confident that new designs would achieve the required standard.

Whilst locomotives were still viewed as the desired traction on main lines, DMUs were seen as a much cheaper alternative to steam power for other services. The Regional bids were for the following 1,993 vehicles out of an eventual total of 5,450.

	ER	LMR	NER	SR	ScR	WR
Powered	79	230	248	18	26	674
Trailer	70	170	248	18	0	212

On the question of what to do with the residue of steam, the Committee felt that this must continue to be used to best advantage. No express and suburban classes were to be built after conclusion of the 1956 building programme. Classes to be selected for withdrawal should be those with only a handful of examples in order to reduce the quantity of spares. Less efficient types should also be identified either for rebuilding or condemnation. The poor state of many sheds meant that money might have to be spent on some as a stop-gap measure.

BR had to provide a freight service that was faster, more reliable and punctual. Improved train marshalling was viewed as one piece in this jigsaw and 55 new yards were planned to replace 150 existing ones. Freight depots and stations were also seen as offering significant scope for rationalisation, with small sites consolidated into larger ones with better facilities.

Reference was made to Britain being the only major country where a sizeable volume of freight was conveyed in unbraked vehicles. This slowed down transit times and caused a less efficient use of track capacity. Catch points were needed at the foot of any gradient steeper than 1 in 260 to deliberately derail unbraked wagons that broke away from a train. Fitting continuous train brakes would enable these points to be eliminated and the Committee recommended the vacuum, not air, system. The choice of system was reviewed subsequently by the Continuous Brakes Committee and the Technical Committee and on 16 February 1956 decided to opt for air braking. Subsequent pressure from the Regions brought a volte face that was to prove costly later with the retro-fitting of train air brake equipment to locomotives.

At the end of the 1955 building programme there would be 1.1 million wagons in stock, of which 606,900 would be used for minerals transportation. The plan was to switch to construction of 24½ -ton wagons from 1957 for this traffic and this would see the stock of this type of wagon reduced to 467,000. By way of commentary, the planned number of vehicles was based on total tonnage but there was no investigation of why so many wagons were needed and whether there was a realistic prospect of increasing wagon productivity. No one bothered to check whether the railways' customers could handle brake-fitted wagons of this size, but more of that anon; yet more examples of bone-headed thinking!

After full implementation of the plan, the total wagon stock was predicted to be 752,000 vehicles. A switch to increased use of containers was foreshadowed but no forecasts were made of the likely affect on merchandise freight activity.

Station reconstruction was admitted to be an outlay without any prospect of extra revenue generation and it was justified on the grounds of passenger expectation for a modern railway. There was a nod towards redevelopment perhaps drawing in non-railway commercial activity but this was not considered further. Stations listed for replacement or reconstruction were Coventry, Edinburgh Waverley, Euston, Glasgow Central, King's Cross, Leeds City, London Bridge, Manchester London Road (later renamed Piccadilly) and Victoria, Newcastle, Peterborough North, Plymouth North Road and York. Five of these were never dealt with, whilst Birmingham New Street is the most significant example omitted from the list that was rebuilt.

Non-gangwayed passenger carriages, which lacked toilets, were to be replaced by DMU and EMU stock. A new pattern of train services and the recasting of timetables was forecast to reduce the number of vehicles needed by 25%. Herein is an admission that, six years after nationalisation, nothing had been done in this area. The total stock of passenger vehicles was given as 42,300, of which 16,500 were over 20 years old and targeted for early withdrawal, and this was to be cut to 36,183. Of course today all Mark 3 (HST) and Mark 4 (ECML) sets and the majority of DMUs and EMUs are over 20 years old. Again, nothing was said about how efficiently the stock was being used.

The report highlights the considerable shipping activity of the Commission, mainly through its packet ports. Services were operated, either directly or in partnership, to Belgium, the Channel Isles, Denmark, France, Ireland, the Netherlands, as well as in estuaries and lakes. Harwich, Dover and Newhaven were identified for port facility upgrading for Continental traffic and Stranraer, Heysham, Holyhead and Fishguard for that to Ireland. As regards estuary sailings, money was to be spent at Gourock, Wemyss Bay, Fairlie Pier, Portsmouth and Fishbourne on the Isle of Wight.

National legislation on health, safety and welfare was in the offing and special provisions appertaining to railways were understood to be included. The Committee therefore made proposals in a range of areas, such as the provision of toilets and washing facilities.

Office mechanisation was not overlooked and the Committee was alive to developments in electronic machines. In fact, provision had been made for the purchase of an 'electronic brain'; how quaint this description of a computer sounds now!

Perhaps the most significant section of the plan comes under the heading of Finance, where the railways were said to represent 74% of the BTC's net assets. The draft covered a proposed outlay of £1.17million between 1956 and 1970, quite a hike over the £500 million contained in the Commission's brief of 14 April.

Of this total, only £300 million was forecast to be available from BTC internal depreciation and maintenance reserves. Additional borrowings of £870 million would be needed, attracting interest of £35 million but the Committee did not believe that this level of interest could be afforded during the currency of the plan, whilst no mention was made of how or when the £870 million could be repaid. The only defence to this situation was to include warm, soothing phrases such as 'the railways are a national necessity' and 'the need to modernise is urgent and immediate'. It was recognised that some (unspecified) assets would be written off before they were life expired and this would increase the railways' costs through added depreciation.

The Plan itself and how it was received, as well as Commission reaction to Watson's Planning Committee report described above, will be considered in the following chapter. As a prelude, a bilateral meeting held on 7 December between MoT and Treasury officials, which predated their sight of the Plan, gives insights into Government thinking. The railways were currently running at a loss and until modernised were unlikely to improve efficiency; benefits of a new charge scheme for freight may bridge the gap in the meantime.

Even so, there was every prospect of a steady increase in Commission accumulated revenue loss and deferring interest charges on borrowing might be a way of giving some help. Treasury officials assumed the Modernisation Plan was technically sound and there was an expectation that the railways would then be able to pay their way. Payment of subsidy to BTC would lead to serious repercussions elsewhere – eg in the coal industry. Clearly the Commission held the sympathy vote in Whitehall.

Chapter 4

The modernisation and re-equipment of British Railways

Planning Committee report reviewed

Sir Daril Watson's Planning Committee report, which was described in the last chapter, was discussed in open session by the Commission on 18 November 1954. Commission members had met in private session previously to consider the document.

The Regional Managers made several comments, judging it unwise to specify within the published Plan the stations to be rebuilt and the lines to be electrified. They recommended an attempt be made to increase demurrage charges. These were levied where wagons were retained during loading and unloading beyond a specified period but were so low as not to serve as a deterrent to wagons being used as storage bunkers, rather than modes of transport. A need for extra technical staff was deemed essential by the Regions.

H. P. Barker was a part-time Commission Member and a senior industrialist in the home appliance sector. He wrote a five-page critique of Watson's report, which he described as 'admirable' but that he had 'serious doubts and substantial criticisms'.

Barker's general criticism was that the report dealt with changing the equipment of the railways but not their operation. His study of the railways had led him to conclude that even perfect equipment would not make them profitable if they were operated as they were then. He added that the Planning Committee's report implied that modernisation would make for long-term viability and he disagreed with this. Barker predicated that evidence would come to light in the next two years that a solid proportion of traffic was grossly uneconomic and that no amount of new equipment would make this so. How far-sighted he was!

Barker felt that, whilst the superstructure of the report was sound, its foundations were in need of radical re-examination. Reginald Wilson had set up a Traffic Costing Service and it had produced figures for passenger services. Barker estimated it would be 18 months before equivalent data on freight would be to hand but he predicted it would show that mineral traffic was subsidising all other carryings. Again he was proved correct.

Criticism was made of wagon utilisation. Currently, this was given as a 10-day turnround, in other words each wagon carried one payload every 10 days.

The Planning Committee forecast this would be cut to seven days by 1970 and Barker regarded this as ludicrous for a modern railway. Just consider how many daily return trips merry-go-round coal trains were making each day during the 1970s and 1980s when pit-to-power station distances were fairly short. Rakes of coal wagons were, on average, making a return trip every 10 days in 1954! The road competition was making even trunk journeys in a two-day round trip.

The decision to have 90mph as the target maximum speed on main lines was queried and Barker judged it should be 100, bearing in mind developments overseas in this direction. Like so much of his critique, he was ignored by the Commission and many main lines were modernised in the 1960s for a 90mph top speed, with locomotives and rolling stock designed accordingly.

One suggestion which was heeded was that the choice of the East Coast for electrification should be reconsidered in favour of the West Coast. Barker felt that the Watson report's basis of electrification using the prevailing standard 1,500V DC system should be reassessed in the light of trials, notably in France, with 50 cycles AC equipment. This was also taken on board and will be described in a later chapter.

Barker was delighted that steam was to be abandoned in favour of diesel, something he had pushed for, for some time. He suggested that trials with contractor-built diesel locomotives over three years could, by 1958, enable large-scale orders to be placed. This is the first reference tracked down in BTC papers to the idea of a Pilot Scheme.

By contrast, the Planning Committee was just proposing the acquisition of 271 machines in line with proposals put forward by the Regions. He counselled against a multiplicity of different types of locomotive but, again, he was not listened to and at great cost in poor reliability and availability and higher maintenance charges.

It cannot be emphasised too much that Barker was an industrialist who had no previous railway experience prior to joining the BTC as a part-time member, whereas Watson's Planning Committee was composed of long-service, full-time railwaymen at the top of their careers. Yet it was Barker who showed far more insight into what was needed to move the railways forward into the second half of the 20th century. A decade later, it was to be another industrialist with no railway experience who was to radically shake up the way BR was run, and who was highly respected by professional railwaymen for what he did. His name was Richard Beeching.

Sir Brian Robertson thanked the Planning Committee for their good work but explained that Commission Members had not yet come to definite conclusions, though there was a wide measure of agreement on the 'technicalities'. He went on to say that the Commission's own Plan would be based on the advice of the Planning Committee and its own appreciation of the future of the transport industry generally and of the economic consequences of the Plan. As a minor critique of Watson's document, Robertson said the BTC's report would 'contain a fuller appreciation of the competence and suitability of the different forms of rail traction now existing, with justification for the types chosen in the Plan'.

Robertson announced the setting up of a small committee of Commission Members, chaired by Sir Reginald Wilson, and with Messrs Pope, Ryan and Valentine, to guide staff in drafting the Plan. They would focus on the report's Introduction, a forecast of the traffics the Plan sought to gain and the economies foreshadowed.

A week later, on the 25th, the Commission unsurprisingly returned to the subject. There was a realisation that there would be an impact on railway works of having to build and maintain diesel and electric traction, and plans for staff retraining would be a consequence of this.

Robertson reported that Members felt there was a need for improved operational methods to make railways competitive in future years, along with the quantity of rolling stock and equipment required for this pattern of operational control. A caveat was to be included in the Plan that requirements for traction were based on best estimates and these could change as a result of the identification of operating efficiencies then being considered.

The BTC meeting on 23 December resolved that Watson was to set up a new planning group to take the Plan forward and deal with the prioritisation of projects; Regional Managers would sit on this group. A week later Sir Reginald Wilson was requested to arrange for the preparation of a statement showing the probable requirements of the Plan in terms of cash year by year and its estimated affect on the Commission's annual financial position. After being sent to the MoT, the Plan was published on 25 January 1955.

The 1955 Plan in detail

Before launching into a description of the '1955 Plan for the Modernisation and Re-equipment of the British Railways', its formal title, it will be useful to set the scene by drawing on the Commission's 1954 report, which was published in 1955 after the release of the Plan.

Writing euphemistically to avoid criticism of the Government, the report referred to 'the easing of restrictions' (that is, Government spending limits) as a result of which the Commission felt able to 'take a broader, bolder and longer-term view of the future role of British Railways'. Reference was made to major technical developments having occurred in recent years, particularly in relation to electric and diesel railway traction, of which British Railways had so far been able to take little advantage.

The 1954 report continued by saying 'In preparing the Plan, it was necessary to ensure that the cost of modernisation was fully justified by the economies it was expected to bring and by the improved revenues to be earned from freight and passenger services which would be speeded up and made more reliable. It was also necessary to consider what were the practical limits on the constructional and manufacturing work which could be carried out within a given number of years.' It will be important to bear these aspirations in mind when the performance of the Plan is reviewed in the next chapter.

A paper read by Commission Member J. C. L. Train to the WR's London Lecture & Debating Society on 6 October 1955 summarised what the BTC was seeking to achieve. Whilst the presentation was undoubtedly tailored for the audience, it gives insights into Commission thinking.

Train took as his theme that industries cannot stand still, they must progress and that the railways' passenger and freight customers had a right to expect better services. He believed these would help win back traffic that was then being carried on overcrowded roads. A key determinant of the Plan's success would be co-operation from staff to get the best out of the new equipment. If the Plan failed, then the railways would decline and jobs would be lost because road and air competition would take traffic away.

Curiously, Train said that the background to the Plan was decentralisation and to encourage railwaymen to take a pride in their jobs. The key element was motive power and steam had had its day. Nuclear power was seen as the fuel of the future for electricity generation and the railways wanted to take advantage of this by pushing through schemes of electrification.

Turning now to the Plan document, the Introduction started by saying that an efficient and modernised railway was essential to the economy of the country, and it should be able to attract and retain sufficient traffic to make it economically self-supporting. Under-investment meant the railways were not operating at full efficiency and the aim of the Plan was to address this. An objective was that the elements should be capable of being started within five years and completed within 15.

Of the £1.2 billion cost, half would be needed to deal with normal replacement of assets, whilst the balance was for updating. Rail was seen as the best mode of transport for the bulk conveyance of passenger and freight, but was not seen as competitive in all sectors, where costs were disproportionately high, and reference was made to the private car. Implementation was estimated to generate a return of at least £85 million on BR's annual turnover of £500 million, a rather startling 17% margin. Passenger services were to be speeded up and their frequency increased. Freight flows were to be recast to offer better trunk flows and less marshalling en route.

Naturally, the document gushed with warm, soothing words about how modernisation would generate public goodwill and have a tonic effect on staff. The Commission felt that the £85 million return took no account of all these social benefits, plus reduced road congestion.

The accompanying table gives a breakdown of the proposed expenditure:

	£m	£m
Freight services		
Construction and reconstruction of 55 marshalling yards, resulting in the total or partial closure of about 150 existing yards.	80	
Reconstruction and mechanisation of freight terminals while closing various old depots, so as to improve transits and speed-up exchange of full-load traffic between road and rail	50	
Associated expenditure on handling equipment and road vehicles.	10	
Provision of continuous brakes on freight stock, thus securing best results from new forms of motive power.	75	
New and improved wagon stock	150	*365*
Passenger carriages and stations		
New passenger carriages, including electric and diesel multiple-unit vehicles and refreshment cars	230	
Improvements to passenger and parcels stations, and carriage-cleaning and servicing depots.	55	*285*
Track and signalling		
Improvements to make possible higher speeds (of at least 100mph on the main lines) and better use of track capacity.	210	

Motive power
Electrification:
Main lines	120	
Suburban (including schemes already authorised)	65	
Dieselisation		
Main lines	125	
Shunting and trip locomotives	25	
Steam motive power depots	10	*345*

Ancillary items
Improvements at the Commission's packet ports	12	
Research & development work	10	
Offices and equipment and staff welfare	13	*35*
Total		*1,240*

To a large degree, these headings drew on the 1953 document drawn up by Harrington's committee and described in the previous chapter, and Watson's Planning Committee report. By virtue of this, there is no benefit in reciting the proposals under each heading here.

Much of the detail within the Planning Committee's report was omitted from the Plan. Suburban routes to be electrified were those on the ER and around Glasgow. Interestingly, the former totalled 200 route miles and the latter 190, the figure that was recommended by the Inglis Report of 1951 mentioned previously. The extent of the scheme was still dependant on agreement with Glasgow Corporation on road and rail services in the area.

Both the East and West Coast routes to Leeds (possibly York) and Birmingham, Liverpool and Manchester respectively were slated for completion during the currency of the Plan, as was the extension of Liverpool Street suburban electrification to Ipswich and branches such as that to Clacton. The report admitted that this was an ambitious programme, which might overstretch the resources of technical staff and manufacturing industry to deliver.

Concerning main line diesel locomotives, the Plan envisaged a rapid changeover from steam to diesel in selected areas. Standardisation of design was the intention, as far as possible. Where possible, line speeds were to be at least 100mph, a change from Watson's Committee proposal and reflecting Barker's opinion.

The Traffic Costing Service had shown that certain stopping and branch-line services were loss-making. Where there was the prospect of winning extra patronage, these would be provided with DMUs, otherwise buses would be substituted.

Efforts were to be made to increase mineral wagon productivity by each wagon spending less time stationary and more time conveying materials. The best the Plan could say on how this would be achieved was through co-operation from customers. The target reduction in turnround time of 30% proposed by Watson's group and so derided by Barker was used as the basis to assess wagon numbers. BR was said to carry a larger quantity of small consignments than many overseas railways and these presented difficulties in achieving improved efficiency.

When it came to implementation, there was inbuilt flexibility in getting projects up and running. It would be for the Regions to work up proposals, drawing on guidance from HQ technical experts. The final decision on priorities and sanction was to rest with the Commission in consultation with the Area Boards.

Implementation of the Plan would not only incur additional interest charges on the loan of £800 million from the Government but would also lead to higher depreciation charges on new, rather than old, equipment and these combined would amount to £80 million. In fact, there was a recognition that advances in technology meant that the new assets would have to be written off more quickly. Steam traction was said to have a life of 40 years but would the same be true for diesels? Coincidentally, the Commission calculated the return on the investment should be £85 million, possibly more, made up of £35 million savings on the passenger side and £60 million on freight but with an adverse £10 million increase in expenses.

Part of the £85 million was derived from a predicted switch of passenger train miles from stopping and branch-line trains to more long-distance and suburban journeys yielding higher returns. Cost savings would accrue from the substitution of steam by diesel and electric traction. Worryingly, the Plan admitted the cost savings appertaining to freight modernisation could not easily be quantified but 'the economic effects are not dissimilar' to those for passenger services. This was because the Traffic Costing Service had not been established long enough to have worked these out. Basically, seven years into nationalisation, BR didn't have a clue about the costs and revenues associated with its freight business!

Even after full implementation, the document admits not all services would be covering even the direct costs of their operation. This was, though, claimed to be a major improvement on the presumed large degree of cross-subsidy between services appertaining in 1954. Current loss-making traffic that modernisation would eventually make profitable would continue to be a drain on Commission resources until the Plan was executed.

Reaction to the Plan

Naturally there was no shortage of comment about the Commission's proposals. The Chancellor of the Exchequer applauded the Plan's 'courageous and imaginative conception'.

In the press, one commentator said that the selection of the West Country as a trial area for the elimination of steam had been predicted and was sensible because of its remoteness from any coalfield. Cornwall, of course, had been selected in 1946 for the conversion of steam locomotives to oil burning.

The *Manchester Guardian* felt that 'the new programme stands for a new spirit which the public will welcome', whilst *The Economist* described it as 'carefully thought out'.

The issue of the *Railway Gazette* for 28 January welcomed the document. It noted that one quarter of the expenditure was earmarked for the replacement of steam and that there was inbuilt flexibility. This was because there was the potential for routes that were to be dieselised initially, be electrified later and the diesels redeployed to displace steam elsewhere. Further credit was given to no stated decision having been taken on the types of diesel, or transmission system.

The editorial lauded the decision to aim for speeds of at least 100mph where conditions were suitable, yet the professional railwaymen chose 90 and it had been an industrialist (H. P. Barker) who argued for at least 100!

Concern was raised at the Commission's confidence in the economic benefit of the Plan being £85 million, which seemed to be based on questionable assumptions. The following week's issue returned more generally to the state of railway finances and the gradual accumulation of deficits, once interest charges were included. This is a subject that will be revisited in a later chapter.

An erudite *Railway Gazette* correspondent wondered why there was no mention of a concurrent switch to electric train heating along with the replacement of steam. The decision to retain steam for carriage heating was to prove an expensive mistake and one the engineers should have appreciated, based on the performance of the steam generators fitted to the prototype diesels. The correspondent then also wondered why the vacuum system had been chosen for train braking, as opposed to compressed air. Again, a short-sighted penny-pinching attitude meant extra cost had to be incurred a decade later in retro-fitting air brake equipment to locomotives.

It was not long before *The Economist* returned to its pre-publication opinion about modernisation. It said 'the mere spending of money does not ensure efficiency; it can be a convenient device for ensuring that inefficiency is chromium-plated'. The periodical considered that there were several ways in which the concept of the Plan might be derailed. One was unimaginative railway management, another was road competition, and finally an unresponsive attitude towards productivity from railwaymen. It continued in the same vein following the May 1955 ASLEF strike by saying that 'the Modernisation Plan would certainly be a waste of money if it attracted nothing more than Luddite indifference from the workforce'.

Over the next five or so years, the number of critics grew, especially concerning the financial justification put forward for some schemes, this in turn hampered by a woebegone approach to working out the cost of moving different types of traffic, even if any costing system existed at all. Further consideration of the efficaciousness of the Plan must wait whilst its implementation is described.

Chapter 5

The Pilot Scheme

Hydraulic vs electric transmission
The first round of Modernisation Plan schemes were announced on 5 May 1955 and one of these was for an order for 171 main line diesels to assess different designs before the placing of large-scale contracts. Although the *Railway Gazette* thought that 11 of the locomotives would have diesel-hydraulic transmission of Continental design, nothing further was known and the periodical thought that invitations to tender for any locomotives had not been issued.

In his talk to the WR London branch in September 1955 referred to in the last chapter, J. C. L. Train considered that most diesels would be of a mixed-traffic design. They would be capable of hauling freight trains at up to 60mph and average 45, whilst mineral trains would travel at up to 55mph and average 40.

During the second half of 1954, the BTC's Technical and Works Committees had been considering the form of the diesel locomotives that might be ordered and the type of transmission to be used within the powertrain. Deutsche Bundesbahn (DB, German Federal Railways) was conducting trials with diesel-hydraulic transmission in main line locomotives of 1,000 and 2,000hp and this provided a counterpoint to the widespread use of diesel-electric powertrains in North America.

As the Commission's CME within the Central Staff, R. C. Bond was naturally following these developments. He produced a memorandum dated 29 September for the Works Committee and this was discussed at its meeting on 6 October, as well as the meeting of the Technical Committee on 14 November. By virtue of the considerable significance of its contents, the document is reproduced here in full:

**DIESEL LOCOMOTIVES WITH HYDRAULIC
TRANSMISSION**

Although, with the exception of the Fell Locomotive operating on the London Midland Region, only electric transmission has so far been fitted to diesel locomotives of over 500hp for British Railways, considerable development has taken place abroad in hydraulic transmission, notably in Germany, where the present policy is to use it in locomotives up to the highest powers in preference to electric transmission.

In this country up to date experience with hydraulic transmission in diesel locomotives is so far confined to eight 200hp light shunting locomotives, ordered from the North British Locomotive Company (NBL). Three of these locomotives, which have the German Voith torque converter transmission made under licence by the North British Locomotive Company, are in service on the North Eastern Region and five more are now under construction for the Scottish Region.

Towards the end of last year, the North British Locomotive Co completed some mixed traffic locomotives, each of 625hp with hydraulic transmission, for the Mauritius Government Railways. A number of test runs with both passenger and freight trains were carried out on the Scottish Region, at one of which I was present. On that occasion two units coupled together worked passenger trains between Glasgow and Edinburgh in a most satisfactory manner.

More recently, the firm have completed preliminary designs and specifications for locomotives in the higher power ranges, which would be suitable for service in this country. I have had a number of informal discussions concerning them with the North British Locomotive Co, who, with a view to assisting their export business, would like to see such locomotives running in regular service on British Railways.

While, as mentioned above, we are obtaining valuable experience with hydraulic transmission in low powered shunting locomotives, such experience is not necessarily valid for locomotives of higher powers. Having regard to the probable extension of diesel traction on British Railways it is, in my opinion, very desirable that trials should be made in this power range because of the potential advantages this form of transmission offers which in relation to electric transmission could eventually be:

1 Reduced weight of locomotive for a given power
2 Lower first cost
3 Reduced maintenance costs.

For such trials to be on a scale which would produce sufficient experience in a reasonably short time I suggest that five locomotives for main line passenger and freight services in the 2,000hp range might be considered, together with six locomotives in the 1,000-1,250hp range to be used as twin units on heavy work or singly for lighter duties. The precise power characteristics to be selected will, of course, be a matter for discussion with the Regions and with the Chief Officers concerned at Headquarters. Such locomotives would be suitable for service very widely throughout British Railways and could form part of any larger scheme involving the use of diesel electric locomotives also.

I therefore RECOMMEND that trials, as suggested above, should be carried out, and, as a first step, approval in principle is sought for the matter to be developed further with the North British Locomotive Co with a view to proposals and estimates of costs being obtained after which I would propose to make a further submission to this Committee. Signed R. C. Bond

This submission did not find unanimous support. Mr Bond's opposite number on the Central Staff, the CEE, S. B. Warder, was not in agreement with his arguments in favour of diesel-hydraulic, and neither was Dr F. Q. den Hollander, the chairman of the board of Netherland Railways, who had been appointed to the Technical Committee as an external advisor. Dr den Hollander was an engineer and an advocate of electric traction and had led the postwar rebuilding of his country's railways.

The Technical Committee meeting of 14 November asked Warder to respond to Bond's memo and he did this by memo dated 13 January 1955, which is also reproduced here. Warder first referred to the potential advantages Bond had ascribed to hydraulic transmission offered, being:

1   Reduced weight of locomotive for a given power.
2   Lower first cost.
3   Reduced maintenance costs.

Quoting Warder on these assertions, they represented 'A statement which I said was in conflict with information that I had obtained recently in America'. This information is summarised in my American Report that has been circulated, and I would therefore only repeat the main facts that, so far as I am aware, represent present generally accepted informed opinion.

1. Of two units having the same horsepower per ton, the one with electric drive can accelerate up to 65 miles per hour more quickly than can the one with hydraulic transmission.
2. The electric transmission can maintain its efficiency over a wider range of speeds than the hydraulic transmission.
3. The reduction in weight claimed for diesel hydraulic locomotives has been mainly obtained from the use of a high-speed engine, since the weight of torque converters, turbine, etc, and additional strengthening usually cancels out the weight of electric generator and traction motors.
4. The diesel-electric type can likewise employ a high-speed engine when it is demonstrated that this is completely reliable and less costly to maintain than the present form.
5. Experience to date with diesel electric locomotives shows that the complete electrical equipment including control circuits is responsible for fewer failures than the engine and ancillary equipment.
6. Hydraulic transmissions make no headway in America for the larger powers despite their vast experience on small powers because no convincing case can be made out on economic, technical or operational grounds.
7. Development of the hydraulic transmission in Germany appears to stem from the experience of shortage of copper (wire for electrical machinery) during previous wars.

It is evident that British Railways – which has not yet committed itself irrevocably to either form of transmission – is interposed geographically between the two fields of development, so that in spite of the above considerations this may be regarded as a good reason for experimenting with hydraulic transmission in order that its performance can be properly equated on a like for like basis with that of the better known electric transmission.

Obviously I would not wish to oppose such experimentation provided a substantial case is proffered, and agree that if a superior transmission system seems a likely possibility, judgement should be suspended pending the result of the authorised trials on hydraulic transmission, and the real cost of maintenance are established.

As a result, the Works Committee gave agreement in principle to Mr Bond's proposals.

During the currency of the above debate, consideration of how a trial of diesel-hydraulic traction might be conducted continued. Another idea that emerged from the Technical Committee meeting on 23 September was a proposal for the importation of a DB Class V200 2,000hp diesel-hydraulic. In truth, importing a German locomotive so soon after the end of the war would have been politically unacceptable but this did not cross the minds of the engineers.

Bond and Keith Grand (the WR's Regional Manager) were charged with looking into this but British loading gauge restrictions ruled it out. As an alternative, Bond proposed that he, and a party comprising Cox, Phillips (the WR Assistant Regional Manager) and R. A. Smeddle (the WR CME) should undertake a fact-finding trip to West Germany in late January/early February 1955. Visits were actually made to the DB, Krauss Maffei (KM designers and builders of Class V200) and Voith (manufacturer of hydraulic transmissions) and other manufacturers.

Representatives from NBL also accompanied the party. The company had a long tradition of steam locomotive construction. It had foreseen the winding down of demand for this form of traction and had no background in electrical equipment and saw German progress with diesel-hydraulic systems as offering a way forward. Licences to build quick-running engines of MAN design and Voith transmissions had enabled the tentative steps in diesel locomotive building referred to above by Bond to be taken. Having a UK builder for German equipment was acceptable politically.

Picking up a couple of threads from the foregoing, it will be noted that WR interest in diesel-hydraulic transmission can be traced back to September 1954. A WR management meeting on 7 October noted the circulation of a scheme for the replacement of steam west of Newton Abbot but referred to the use of diesel-electrics, not diesel-hydraulics.

Phillips had been a member of Watson's modernisation Planning Committee and the chairman of the Forms of Motive Power sub-committee. The WR had been the first Region to propose a trial of main line diesel traction in a discrete area and this made sense to the engineers. Cox has commented that, unlike the other Big Four railways, the GWR had no serious experience with electric traction and, aside from the power equipment in its two prototype gas turbine locomotives, Swindon was not equipped in a significant way to maintain electrical machines. The mechanical engineers wanted to try hydraulic drive and the WR was the obvious and willing place to do this. In other words, it was not the WR that instigated the idea of using diesel-hydraulic drivetrains in main line locomotives but the BR Central Staff.

Concerning events in Germany at this time, DB was coy about giving details of 'V200' performance and none of the five prototypes had either MAN engines or Voith transmission, the types for which NBL had licences. Both manufacturers did, though, have equipment installed in DB traction around this time. Writing about the British delegation's German trip, Cox said the 'V200s' were 'certainly running a railway'. A key to the successful operation of the DB's locomotives was the use of a very limited number of carefully trained drivers.

On 17 February 1955 the BTC agreed in principle to an order to NBL for five 2,000hp and six 1,000hp locomotives (the NBL 11). This was in line with Bond's proposal of the previous September, which had arisen from his dialogue with NBL going back to December 1953. These talks were not recorded in any committee minutes before September 1954 and so perhaps Bond was not so anti-diesel as he is often portrayed! Indeed, he was clearly fully informed of developments in Britain and Germany. These orders pre-dated by many months other contracts placed under the Pilot Scheme.

Decisions on diesel-electrics

Concurrent with the debate about hydraulic transmission, the engineers were drawing up plans for an initial batch of orders for diesel-electric locomotives. Although the LMR, SR and WR had signalled interest to the Planning Committee in acquiring a total of 271 locomotives as a first wave away from steam, the engineers were thinking more in line with Commission Member Barker in terms of a programme of orders from different manufacturers to permit an assessment of performance and reliability.

Discussions were also taking place on the power ranges of diesels to be ordered, with a memo from Commission Member Train of 15 September starting the ball rolling. A memo of 11 November from Harvey, Bond and Warder was submitted to the Works Committee setting out a proposal.

First, the memo said it would be for the Operating Department to draw up requirements but that this would involve extended discussions with the Regions and this would be too protracted for the ordering of initial prototypes.

Next, it was pointed out that the types of locomotive that could be built was constrained by the diesel engines that were available from approved suppliers. In order for the Operating Department to gain experience as quickly as possible of the capabilities of diesel traction on a wide range of traffic types, the three writers suggested locomotives be acquired in three power groups:

Original designation	Later designation	HP	Duties
A	1	600-800	Pick-up and cross-country freight
B	2	1,000-1,250	General mixed traffic
C	4	Above 2,000	Heavy main line services

All the designs were to be fitted for working in multiple and the writers thought there might be circumstances when the use of two smaller locomotives could be better than one large one. Locomotives could be built with either one or two power units; the 'V200s' had two engines, each of 1,000bhp.

The writers judged the reliability and availability of the existing main line prototypes as leaving 'something to be desired'. They therefore wanted orders placed with as wide a range of manufacturers of engines and transmissions as possible. Ultimately, however, they wanted as much standardisation as possible in order to minimise manufacturing and running costs and also to permit inter-Regional working. Type 2 was seen as the category which would be the largest numerically.

The above memo was discussed at the Works Committee meeting on 17 November and the writers' recommendation for the issuing of invitations to tender for 20 Type 1, 80 Type 2 and 10 Type 4 complete locomotives from contractors was agreed. Additionally, 20 Type 2s and 10 Type 4s were to be built in BR's own shops, resulting in 110 examples from industry and 30 built in-house. The Regions argued that the power band for Type 1 was inadequate and so 20 further examples of 1,000hp were added by the meeting, making 160 in total.

The foregoing enables some conclusions to be drawn. First, the power bands were based not on traffic requirements but the outputs of diesels that the engineers considered could be supplied by industry. Thus Type 2 equated roughly to Class 4 steam traction, whereas (except on the SR) Class 5 was numerically the largest. This also means the engineers already had an eye on the likely outcome of the initial orders, purely because they knew what was being manufactured in the UK.

On 26 November Train and Barker visited EE's works and saw that company's high-power prototype, *Deltic*, under construction. They discussed the potential of the opposed-piston Deltic engine for rail applications, it having seen extensive Royal Navy use. The EE prototype was being fitted with two 16-cylinder engines, each capable of 1,650bhp, but others of 800, 1,100 and 2,200bhp were available. Reporting on the visit to the Technical Committee on 8 December, the meeting recommended that ten examples of Type 2 should have a single 1,100bhp Deltic unit. These quick-running engines would allow a comparison to be made with the MAN engines of NBL manufacture intended for the diesel-hydraulic designs that had been agreed in principle by the Works Committee.

The same meeting felt the best approach to the issuing of invitations to tender was to route these through the Locomotive Manufacturers Association, which could forward these to companies able to design and build locomotives in different power categories. Trials of these locomotives was to last three years and, as far as possible, a common form of control system across all manufacturers was to be adopted to facilitate multiple operation.

On 13 January 1955 the Technical Committee returned to the topic of the EE prototype *Deltic* and agreed that facilities should be granted for it to operate in normal railway service. Other matters discussed were the need to standardise designs, that the first orders of diesels under the Modernisation Plan should be evaluated in three years, and that the view of the Regional Managers was that the performance of the early main line prototypes had been 'disappointing'.

On 2 February the Works Committee reviewed the locomotive building and condemnation programme for 1956. Each year, plans were drawn up for locomotive and rolling stock construction and withdrawal both in the railway's own works and for orders to be placed with contractors. Within the programme were included proposals for the purchase of the NBL 11 already referred to, and 10 2,000hp diesel-electrics from contractors, plus 10 Type 4s from BR's shops. Interestingly, the introductory period with the diesel-hydraulics was described as 'experimental', which meant there would be no matching condemnation of steam locomotives but this did not apply to the diesel-electrics.

The same meeting also proposed the completion of the RE's five-stage building programme of 1951 for diesel shunters. This covered 92 of the BR/EE standard 350hp examples and 50 of 200hp from contractors.

Freight and mixed-traffic steam power of Classes 9F, 5MT, 4 and 2 tender locomotives and Class 4 tank locomotives to a total of 227 was for allocation to all Regions. Of significance is that none of the '9Fs' were for the WR.

The BTC agreed these proposals on 17 February. To avoid upsetting the railway unions, care was to be taken in the publicity given to the ordering of diesels from contractors. Despite the ER's input into the Forms of Motive Power Sub-Committee declaring that 2,000hp diesels would be inadequate for hauling East Coast line expresses, the 10 now sanctioned from contractors were to be based on the Region. The 10 to be built by the railways were to be based on the LMR, whilst the NBL 11 would go to the WR.

On 24 March, the Commission gave outline approval for the balance of 140 locomotives proposed by the Works Committee under the Pilot Scheme, making for a total of 171 and allocated to the 1956, 1957 and 1958 building programmes.

The following month the MoT met with the Treasury and the plans for the Pilot Scheme were outlined. It was explained that the aim was to gain experience, especially in maintenance costs, before building 2,500 diesels during the period of the Plan. A 'small number' were to be built by British Railways to gauge costs and also for experience.

At the 11 March meeting, the Commission attempted to put in place arrangements for co-ordinating the work of Central Staff officers in compiling information about locomotive build and delivery schedules with the Regions and their requirements for area schemes for conversion to diesel traction. The Central Staff would have decided on a range of standard types and the Region would then select the ones that were most suitable for each scheme. This was to culminate in a huge document describing passenger trains of the future which was produced in 1957 and will be considered in a later chapter.

Meanwhile, the Technical Committee had been debating the question of how modern traction should heat trains. F. Q. den Hollander, the chairman of Netherlands Railways and a Committee Member, drew on experience not only with his own railway but also in running trains across frontiers into neighbouring countries. He said electric locomotives should only have electric train heating (ETH) equipment. He counselled that steam generators were costly and difficult to maintain. Den Hollander added that freight motive power would not need train heating equipment. Finally, he said DMUs with underfloor engines should have self-contained heating provision for each carriage.

Separate vans containing a steam generator were deemed impractical because of the large number of trains that joined or split en route. The engineers judged that sufficient space could be included in locomotives to permit the retro-fitting of an electric generator for train supply.

What comes across in this debate is how little British Railways' engineers understood diesel traction. They should have known how the early prototypes had suffered problems with their steam generators and how space within locomotives was very limited, particularly due to the British loading gauge. Steam train heating was to be another issue that would later prove to be a thorn in the side of diesel reliability and availability.

Keeping Swindon busy
With Derby Works busy designing 10 Type 4s and 20 Type 2s and the British

locomotive industry occupying itself with the tender documents for the 141 other locomotives in the Pilot Scheme, developments were taking place on the WR. Philips, the Region's Assistant Regional Manager, had been part of the team that had gone to Germany two months before and seems to have reported very favourably on diesel-hydraulic traction. Compared to the prototype diesel-electrics, which weighed of the order of 130 tons, the German 'V200s' of 2,000hp turned the scales at 80 tons, equal to a saving in excess of a coach in weight.

Here the events get murky. It is not known whether the WR knew at this stage that the 2,000hp design being worked up by NBL would turn out to be around 115 tons, still a coach heavier than the 'V200s'. The Region seems to have decided it wanted to build its own diesel-hydraulics and a dialogue was in progress with an alternative German supplier of powertrains.

At its meeting on 11 March 1955 the Works Committee learned that progress was being made with the Maybach company of Germany for up to three powertrains of the type that were being used in the 'V200s'. Maybach said drawings would be supplied and the WR CM&EE considered Swindon could build the locomotives. Grand claimed the total cost of a Swindon-built, Maybach-equipped locomotive would be £72,000 and so less than NBL's quote of £86,000. He also argued that it would be advantageous for NBL to have competition.

Several issues emerge from this. Did Maybach approach the WR or vice versa? Did Grand see this as a device for keeping Swindon busy, as can be claimed with the decision to order 200 Class 94XX tank engines for heavy shunting, the building of which was ending? The decision to order the NBL 11 was viewed as an experiment, so what was the rationale to extend the experiment if not for Swindon's benefit? Events proved Grand had been way too optimistic in his estimate of building costs and his CM&EE likewise in the difficulties Swindon would experience in design and construction.

Having debated the issues, the Works Committee asked the Commission on 26 May to give approval in principle to the purchase of three sets of equipment of Maybach design but subject to manufacturing taking place in the UK. It was emphasised that this was an experimental project and took the total number of locomotives to be ordered under the Pilot Scheme to 174, and these three locomotives were to be part of the 1957 Building Programme.

Contrary to what the Germans had said, progress was protracted in finding licensees to build Maybach's engines and that company's transmissions, which were marketed under the name Mekydro. The BTC meeting on 22 September was informed by Bond that the licensing issue remained unresolved and permission was given to buy direct from Maybach. The Publicity Officer was to be kept in touch with developments because of the anticipated public criticism of buying German and the howls of protest from the Locomotive Manufacturers Association. Eventually two UK engineering companies agreed to become licensees for engine and drivetrain manufacture.

Then the issue of the design of the mechanical parts of the 'V200' had to be dealt with. Whilst Maybach might have said plans would be provided, no one seems to have understood that these did not cover the bodywork and bogies and that these had been produced by KM. The latter was willing to grant a licence to the WR but on payment of a royalty based on the number of locomotives built. KM supplied plans in German and eventually Swindon overcame the issue of translation by bringing a German employee off the shop floor at Swindon into the drawing office, where he stayed for a number of years.

No one on the WR appeared to have appreciated what was involved in aspects of KM's design. This did not use a traditional strength underframe but instead mirrored aircraft and airship principles of a stressed body skin as an element within load bearing of the overall structure. Overall weight was saved and this was a key reason for the 'V200's' overall weight of only 80 tons. Stressed-skin construction was by no means straightforward and it has been suggested that Swindon struggled to get to grips with what was involved.

Eventually Swindon built 38 examples of what became the 'D800' (Class 42) or 'Warship' class, whilst NBL built 33 but fitted with MAN and Voith powertrains. Before this, the true cost of constructing this design emerged. Far from the £72,000 Grand had told the BTC, the amount was over £100,000 and thus not only way above the £86,000 of the first five NBL examples but also the £90,000 of the 2,000hp diesel-electrics ordered from EE under the Pilot Scheme. It was the scale of these costs, and those of Swindon's follow-on design, which debunked the claim that diesel-hydraulics were in principle always cheaper to build than diesel-electrics.

Grand and Smeddle also overlooked another issue. The 'V200s' were used mainly on light passenger trains but the WR would have to deploy its Class 42s on freight. The vast majority of freight vehicles were unbraked, which meant that the role of the locomotive in braking the train was very important. Experience found that the small wheel diameter of KM's bogie design couldn't cope with dissipating the friction-generated heat of the braking effort and this limited the utility of a nominally mixed-traffic design. Nevertheless, Grand's push for the project kept Swindon busy, and hang the implications!

Tender evaluation

A memo of 29 September 1955 gives the details of the responses received by the Commission from industry to its invitation to tender. Sixteen companies submitted some 200 bids. In appraising the results lowest price was not always the overriding factor in the decision because the Works Committee was keen to evaluate the output of different manufacturers and also different designs. It had already been decided that the 160 diesel-electric locomotives would be based on either the ER or the LMR.

As noted above, an order for 10 Type 4s had already gone to EE, which was perhaps unsurprising because it had provided the powertrains for Nos 10000/1 and 10201-3. The 10 BR-built Type 4s were to be equipped with Swiss-based Sulzer Bros engines manufactured under licence in Britain. Sulzer Bros was a world-class company with a high reputation for diesel engines for rail applications dating back to the 1930s. All the Type 4s were to have a cab at each end and a top speed of 90mph.

Of the 40 Type 1 locomotives to be ordered, 20 were to come from EE and be equipped with an eight-cylinder version of the 16-cylinder traction unit fitted in No 10203, as well as in the 10 new Type 4s from that company. The other 20 were to have an 800bhp Davey Paxman Co diesel, the same company that had supplied the engine for the prototype No 10800. Half of these were to come from NBL and the others from British Thomson Houston, the latter subcontracting construction to the Yorkshire Engineering Co. All the Type 1s were to have only one cab.

The Type 2s were to have a cab at each end and a 75mph top speed, the latter surprising in the light of earlier thinking that two of this class could be used in place of a single 90mph Type 4. The engines chosen were to come from manufacturers whose products were already in use either at home or abroad.

Part of the reason for ordering engines from Crossley, a company normally associated with buses than railways, was that Irish Railways had ordered a similar design, which had followed an enquiry from its CM&EE (no less than Oliver Bulleid!) enquiry of the Admiralty as to the performance of the same engines in marine service. Even before the Irish contract, a small number of Crossley-powered locomotives had been built by Metropolitan-Vickers for Western Australia. In fact a number of diesel shunters already in traffic on the LMR were equipped with Crossley engines and these had given trouble. Accordingly, the Works Committee wanted a guarantee of satisfactory performance for the 1,200bhp units now to be ordered.

Another facet of the Works Committee's decision to order from Crossley was a desire to try out a diesel running on the two-stroke cycle, whereas the vast majority of large diesels are four-stroke machines. General Motors, of course, had adopted two-stroke as the basis for its traction range, at this date Model 567.

Following from the Technical Committee's interest in the Deltic engine, also a two-stroke, it was unsurprising that an order for 10 locomotives with this prime mover were ordered.

J. F. Harrison, the CM&EE of the LMR, was interested in engines of Sulzer design, viewing these as more sophisticated than those of EE. Thus the Type 2s to be built at Derby were to have a six-cylinder version of the Model 12LDA28 unit destined for its Type 4s.

Another interesting decision was to recommend an order should go to NBL to build 10 diesel-electric versions of the six diesel-hydraulic Type 2s already agreed for the WR. This was stated to be with a view of offering a clear, direct comparison between the two types of transmission.

Table 5 Pilot Scheme orders

BHP	TOPS Class	Number series	Main contractor	Engine	Trans-mission	No	Re-order
Type 1							
800	15	D8200-9	BTH	Paxman	BTH	10	Yes
800	16	D8400-9	NBL	Paxman	GEC	10	No
1,000	20	D8000-19	EE	EE	EE	20	Yes
Type 2							
1,000	21	D6100-9	NBL	MAN	GEC	10	Yes
1,000	22	D6300-5	NBL	MAN	Voith	6	Yes
1,100	23	D5900-9	EE	Deltic	EE	10	No
1,160	24	D5000-19	BR	Sulzer	BTH	20	Yes
1,160	26	D5300-19	BRCW	Sulzer	CP	20	Yes
1,200	28	D5700-19	MV	Crossley	MV	20	No
1,250	30	D5500-19	Brush	Mirrlees	Brush	20	Yes
Type 4							
2,000	40	D200-9	EE	EE	EE	10	Yes
2,000	41	D600-4	NBL	MAN	Voith	5	No
2,000	42	D800-2	BR	Maybach	Mekydro	3	Yes
2,300	44	D1-10	BR	Sulzer	CP	10	Yes
		Total				*174*	

BRCW = Birmingham Railway Carriage & Wagon, BTH = British Thomson Houston, Brush = Brush Bagnall, CP = Crompton Parkinson, EE = English Electric, MV = Metropolitan-Vickers, NBL = North British Locomotive Company

Although overseas builders had submitted bids, none were accepted. General Motors (including its Australian subsidiary, Clyde Engineering Co) and the American Locomotive Co (including its Canadian associate, Montreal Locomotive Works) offered fast delivery but only their standard designs which would not fit the British loading gauge. General Electric of the USA offered to design bespoke to the British loading gauge but, as was also true of the other overseas contractors, when import duty was added the prices were up to 40% above comparable indigenous competitors.

The Works Committee sanctioned the placing of orders on 12 October but a month was to elapse before orders were signed due to negotiations with the contractors over the contract conditions. In hindsight, it is hard to argue against the thinking behind the Pilot Scheme orders. The outcome of the plan turned out to be another matter.

By June 1956 the question of the Regional allocation of the Pilot Scheme locomotives had been debated and it was agreed that the best results would be gained by the elimination of steam in discrete areas, as had been discussed in the committee stage of the Plan in 1954. Thus Derby's Type 4s were all to be based at Crewe, whilst the EE equivalents were to be given to Stratford and Hornsey for Great Eastern and East Coast duties.

Stratford was also to receive the Brush Type 2s, whilst those from BRCW, EE and NBL were to be allocated to Hornsey for King's Cross suburban work. Derby's Type 2s were to join their larger cousins at Crewe and the Metrovicks were for Midland main line diagrams based at Derby.

Type 1s were to be sent to East London sheds on the ER and LMR to hasten the end of steam and assuage London County Council's barracking about locomotive pollution.

Chapter 6

Diesel multiple units

Also in the first announcement of Modernisation Plan schemes was the ordering of 844 vehicles (power cars and trailers) for DMUs. BTC approval in principal for the construction of 858 power cars and 550 trailers had actually been given on 16 December 1954, which predated Ministerial approval of the Plan and for quantities slightly at variance with the May 1955 announcement.

The decision created an allocation against which Regions could bid for particular schemes, some of which had already been agreed and some that were still being drawn up. It was expected that deliveries were to be completed within two years.

It is worth exploring here how the advantages of DMUs over steam were espoused in a memorandum of June 1954 prepared for the Central Transport Consultative Committee. Twelve were identified:

- Fuel costs per ton mile were lower;
- Different train formations could be assembled for specific areas of operation;
- Reduced wear and tear on the permanent way by virtue of lower axle loads and the elimination of hammer blow from the driving wheels saves money;
- Faster acceleration permitting shorter journey times;
- Absence of variation in tractive effort by having power spread across several vehicles;
- Elimination of the need for turntables and engine release roads, also reducing costs and speeding-up turn-round times at journey's end;
- When operated in conjunction with bus fleets, common engines and transmissions reduce spare parts holdings;
- Units may be changed very rapidly giving power cars a very good availability;
- Power cars can be put into service very quickly, even after being stabled for several days, whereas a steam locomotive requires many hours to get up steam from cold;
- Running costs are reduced by there being no requirement for a fireman;

- Running sheds are less polluting to the local environment and are much cleaner places of work;
- Diesel engine coolant can be circulated to provide carriage heating and so increase the efficiency of the power car as a whole.

In hindsight, some of these now look illusory. Curiously, one of the biggest benefits from the public's standpoint was the enhanced journey experience because of a cleaner, lighter carriage interior and superior external views.

Some of the schemes dealt with in Chapter 3 were covered by the announcement, namely inter-city trains for Edinburgh to Glasgow and Birmingham to Swansea, plus schemes in Lincolnshire and East Anglia. In addition, the NER received sanction for Newcastle to Carlisle and Newcastle to Sunderland and Middlesbrough, whilst the LMR was to introduce DMUs from Manchester to Marple and Macclesfield and on branches in North Wales, between Birmingham and Lichfield and other local services. Of these, the Manchester scheme was the largest announced to date and comprised 168 power cars and 116 trailers. Train mileage was forecast to rise by 38%. The SR was to get its first DMUs with inter-city sets for London to Hastings and cross-country sets for Hampshire, these will be described in more detail below.

Reorganisation of BR into area boards arising out of the 1953 Transport Act brought a complete review of passenger requirements and schemes for the widespread introduction of DMUs. During 1954 the BUT 150hp and the Rolls Royce six-cylinder 180hp engines were available and these higher powers made it unnecessary to construct all railcars in the relatively more expensive light alloy. This brought a switch to steel instead for orders placed with contractors, though Derby continued with its lightweight design until August 1956.

On 15 September 1955 the BTC authorised a further 1,392 vehicles, which were not for any specific schemes at that date but could be bid for by the Regions. At its meeting on 31 January 1957 the Commission envisaged that all branch and cross-country passenger services should be either covered by DMUs or railbuses or withdrawn by the end of 1961. The aim was cost reduction and the elimination of steam.

DMU procurement was considered again on 21 February when a further tranche of vehicles – 152 motor coaches and 148 trailers – was given outline approval. This adopted the recommendation from the Works Committee meeting on the 11th which proposed these as an interim step until a full estimate of the number of DMUs required until 1962 had been derived. Concerning performance capabilities, the Works Committee considered that all requirements could be met by the use of a range of engines of between 150 and 200bhp, when matched to the required mix of motor and trailer vehicles.

John Ratter, the Technical Advisor in the General Staff, explained to the Commission at its 21 February 1955 meeting that a report was being prepared on the policy for new designs and the materials to be used with particular reference to the power/weight ratio of the set as a whole. Robertson, the BTC Chairman, said the report should give not only the comparative construction costs but also the estimated operating and maintenance figures and should advise the Commission of the best type of vehicles for its needs. If change was recommended, the report should say when it should be introduced into the existing production programme, without forgetting the importance of avoiding delay in carrying out this vital part of the Plan.

Robertson continued that endeavour should be made to satisfy the traction requirements of the Regions, and they should see that DMUs were not overloaded by hauling tail traffic, which should only be attached in exceptional circumstances. The provision of luggage accommodation immediately behind the driver's seat in some vehicles was mentioned and Ratter confirmed that there were no technical reasons why luggage should not be accommodated elsewhere to give passengers in the front seats a better view ahead.

The report referred to by Ratter was finally produced in November 1957 and was a collaboration involving the British Railways Central Staff and Regional Managers. It proposed standard types of DMU and EMU, with standardised layouts and reduced variations in types of 'cross-country' (low-density) DMUs. Even now, the WR held out for a different design from the rest! At that date there were 53 types of high-density (suburban) DMU and EMU vehicles and the plan was now to standardise on just 16, excluding Inter-City and Glasgow suburban.

The existing inter-city sets on the Glasgow-Edinburgh and Birmingham-Swansea routes comprised five vehicle types and were the same length as the standard hauled coach at 63ft 6in. Sets for the Glasgow to Ayr and Girvan route then on the drawing board and based on the earlier series of inter-city DMUs were to be the subject of some modifications.

A long gap had occurred between the outline approval for the above inter-city sets, which were described in Chapter 3, and the announcement of the commencement of their construction. Michael Bonavia puts this, and delays with further Derby Lightweight DMUs, down to Regional bickering over modifications to designs to meet real or imaginary requirements. This also comes across in the November 1957 report on DMU vehicle types. Perhaps a dominant, centrally-controlling Railway Executive was not so bad after all!

DMU design

There were three basic types of DMU, suburban, branch and local, and finally cross-country. Suburban sets were formed of one, three or four vehicles, whilst branch and local ones were of two- or three-car formations. Cross-country DMUs had three vehicles and provision was included for buffet facilities. Two-car formations normally had one motor coach and one trailer but a few had both vehicles powered for duties in very hilly areas. Three-car sets had two motor coaches and one trailer, whilst four-car formations had two vehicles of each type.

Vehicles in suburban sets had 2+3 seating and doors at each seating position. Branch and local service vehicles also had 2+3 seating but only two doors per side per vehicle. Finally, the cross-country vehicles had 2+2 seating and also two doors per side.

Although the majority of DMUs employed a powertrain comprising two BUT 150bhp diesels and a four-speed epicyclic gearbox mounted under each motor coach, alternative powertrains were fitted in a number of cases. Rolls Royce engines of 180 and 238bhp were used where extra power per set was required. The company had a licence to manufacture a hydraulic drive designed by the Twin Disc Clutch Co of the USA, which had developed the old Lysholm-Smith type of torque converter whose upgrading Leyland Motors had abandoned in the 1940s. The standard diesel-mechanical multiple unit was limited to 70mph, but certainly in later years the Rolls Royce/Twin Disc diesel-hydraulics were permitted 75.

One application where the Rolls-Royce C8N 238bhp engines were matched with the Twin-Disc torque converter was the Derby-built four-car suburban sets for use out of St Pancras on local services to Bedford. For a train weight of 136 tons, the installed power was 952hp. These sets had to contend with an operating regime that called for relatively short start-to-stop schedules demanding full-power acceleration, where hydraulic drive gave a better tractive effort characteristic than a mechanical equivalent, together with some longer spells of flat-out running. Some trains made a final call at Harpenden and then had to complete a 20-mile, mainly downgrade, dash for London in 20 minutes. It was perhaps unsurprising that some technical issues arose but these were resolved and the DMUs survived until electrification in the mid-1980s.

Some of the two-car branch line DMUs received two Albion engines of 230bhp per set in order to offer better performance than could be obtained from two standard 150bhp diesels. Perhaps surprisingly, the Swindon-built three-car cross-country DMUs retained the standard powertrain and the extra weight of the vehicles over that of other designs gave an inferior power-to-weight ratio in consequence.

Railway workshops did not monopolise DMU construction, with a number of contractors winning orders. External styling seems to have been left to the builders and Swindon's cross-country sets were judged to reflect a significant improvement in external appearance from its first inter-city offering.

Railbuses

Despite seeing at first hand the extensive use of four-wheeled diesel-powered passenger vehicles on the Continent during its research, the 1952 Lightweight Trains Committee rejected the concept for British Railways. By not having bogies, such carriages were lighter and smaller than the GWR-pattern of railcar and thus had a lower carrying capacity in order to come within the low axleload constraints of most branch lines. Another factor would then have been insufficient capacity to handle parcels and the, so-called, freight 'sundries' traffic that was still a feature of branch traffic.

As the 1950s wore on, increasing focus was placed on loss-making, mainly rural, passenger services. The approach taken was to determine how the same railway could be run more economically, rather than whether a different approach to railway operation might offer the best option, if the meagre traffic offering was at all viable for rail-borne transportation. With so much of its network clearly loss-making, the Scottish Area Board was particularly concerned with the prospect of service withdrawals.

An Unremunerative Passenger Services Committee was set up, whilst Commission Member Sir Reginald Wilson wrote a paper entitled 'Finance and the Stopping Passenger Train'. Thus it was that on 27 September 1956 the BTC gave outline approval for an experiment with railbuses and all Regions bar the SR would participate. After the usual process of proposed schemes from the Regions and tender appraisal by the Works Committee, 22 vehicles were ordered from five manufacturers, one of which was German and had extensive experience of this type of motive power.

Robertson referred to the forthcoming railbus experiment in a press briefing about modernisation in March 1957. Although the five contractors continued with production, Regional bickering over design aspects did not see final plans produced until November, yet deliveries began in February 1958. One idea to have the driver as the solitary traincrew, with responsibility for ticket-issuing, was scotched.

Even as the vehicles began to arrive, mounting BTC losses brought ever more draconian attitudes towards the rural railway. Drawing on year-end figures contained in the BTC annual reports, the number of stations on the first day of nationalisation in 1948 was 8,294, compared to 6,729 in 1962, with total route miles cut during the same period from 19,639 to 17,471. These changes therefore pre-date the impact of Dr Richard Beeching's Reshaping Report of 1963. In that report, whilst the cost-saving benefit of railbuses was acknowledged, it was judged to be insubstantial and inadequate to be the hoped-for saviour of large sections of the rural railway.

The GWR had proved that diesel railcars were a useful form of traction on a number of branch services and, in hindsight, it is surprising that the Lightweight Trains Committee rejected the railbus concept in 1952. On balance, though, the advent of wider car ownership as the 1950s turned into the 1960s, coupled with the much cheaper option of the subsidised road bus, meant that the routes for which the railbus was conceived were doomed, even if they had arrived five years earlier and had enjoyed a longer period to hold or win back traffic.

WR schemes

To be fair to the WR, the proposals it submitted to the Works Committee for modernisation schemes were the most detailed and it is worth looking at those ones for Birmingham and Bristol.

The Birmingham proposal was made in two parts, the first in 1955 and the second in 1957, and covered the WR routes passing through Snow Hill or terminating at Moor Street, plus those in the Black Country, that is Wolverhampton and Dudley. Some trains were, however, to cover diagrams as far as Oxford and Didcot, Bewdley, Worcester and Wellington (Salop). Phase 1, comprising 58 DMU vehicles, was sanctioned by the Commission on 23 June 1955. On 7 January 1957 the WR made a submission to the Works Committee for Phase 2 for a further 49 vehicles. These were required in order to complete dieselisation of the local and suburban services, save for certain rush-hour and unremunerative operations which were to remain steam-powered.

The rolling stock for both phases was to come from the Commission's authorisation of 15 September 1955 for 1,392 vehicles. The breakdown by vehicle type for the 107 examples was as follows:

Suburban 3-car		Cross-country		Single units		Driving vehicles	
M	T	M	T	M	T	M	T
			Required for traffic				
46	23	6	3	5	0	0	1
			Spare vehicles				
12	6	2	1	2	0	0	0

Overall total 107 vehicles, M=motor, T=trailer

A requirement for spare vehicles equal to 21% of the total now appears very high. Deliveries were to begin in spring 1957 for the Phase 1 vehicles. For a total outlay of £1,446,403, a saving of £215,000 per annum was forecast, derived by the elimination of 40 steam locomotives, five ex-GWR railcars, 142 coaches, one driver, 72 firemen, one guard and two shunters. Even so, an excess of £130,000 of costs over receipts was forecast and this was despite a predicted 10% uplift in revenue as a direct result of dieselisation.

Tyseley diesel depot had been authorised in 1955 and was to handle all maintenance above daily inspections. Facilities for fuelling and inspection were to be provided at Wolverhampton Cannock Road, Stourbridge and Leamington Spa.

The Bristol Area DMU scheme (this differentiates it from the dieselisation of main line locomotives, under which the West of England was Area 1 and Bristol Area 2) was dated 27 March 1957 and covered services from there to Bath Spa, Taunton, Avonmouth, Severn Beach and Pilning Low Level via Clifton Down, Pilning Low Level via Filton, Avonmouth Dock via Henbury as well as Westbury to Bath Spa, Swindon to Bath Spa, Chippenham to Westbury via Melksham, Westbury to Weymouth, Maiden Newton to Bridport and finally Chippenham to Calne. An annual saving of £87,000 per annum was estimated for a scheme covering suburban, cross-country and rural workings.

Motive power requirements comprised:

Type		Motor	Trailer
Suburban	3-car	18	9
	2-car	8	0
Trailers		2	
Cross-country	3-car	30	15
	2-car	10	0
Trailers		1	

The above was estimated to cost £1.3 million and three suburban and four cross-country sets were included as maintenance spares. The vehicles were to come from the total of 1,392 authorised by the BTC on 15 September 1955. Resources displaced comprised 28 steam locomotives, two ex-GWR railcars, 135 coaches, 68 firemen, 15 shed staff and 19 carriage servicemen.

Maintenance was to be carried out at a new facility at Bristol Marsh Junction, with fuelling and inspection facilities at Bristol Dr Days Sidings, Westbury and Weymouth. Closure of the steam sheds at Bath Spa and Bridport was under consideration.

Suburban services around Bristol had been recast to a regular-interval pattern in January 1955 and these were to be unaltered by the change in motive power. Elsewhere, a regular-interval and accelerated timetable was to offer improvements. In conjunction with the SR Hampshire Area scheme, trains between Bristol and Portsmouth were to be accelerated by up to 66 minutes. Annual mileages run under the proposed scheme were 2.4 million, an increase of 700,000.

In terms of revenue growth, it was admitted that Bristol and its hinterland were well served by intensive bus services, against which rail was competing, but a 'nominal' increase of 5% in receipts was included. Unlike the Birmingham Area scheme, no comment was made concerning the overall commercial viability of the Bristol proposals, just an estimate of savings and a passing comment to the effect that services would still not be fully remunerative.

These two schemes highlight some of the issues which arose out of the Modernisation Plan. Although both excluded services under review by the Unremunerative Passenger Services Committee (for which records do not survive in the National Archives), neither would bring about the overall viability of the services in question. Then there must also be a question mark over the way the financial estimates of costs were drawn up because it appears highly likely that no allowance for costs other than those directly attributable to the running of the trains was included. In other words, were station running costs and Divisional, Regional and BTC HQ elements, as well as interest on the money borrowed to finance DMU purchase, covered?

Also worthy of note is the remark that suburban trains in Bristol were competing with local buses, whose operation was subsidised by Bristol Corporation. Was it sensible to run two competing publicly-subsidised services? The answer to that question came in the 1960s when all routes bar that from Bristol to Severn Beach were axed.

Sadly, as was to be found time and again, modernisation did not turn losses into profits. When the LMR carried out a 'back check' (a term used by the

Commission to refer to the retrospective re-examination of the financial impact of modernisation schemes) only its Birmingham to Leicester DMUs were profitable and this came as a shock.

SR DEMUs

The SR took a different course from all the other Regions in its motive power provision for non-electrified inter-urban and cross-country services.

By 1955 it became necessary to take urgent steps to meet increasing public pressure for the improvement of train services on the line between London and Hastings via Tunbridge Wells. This is a line containing many sharp curves and steep gradients, which impose numerous slacks in the running speeds. Two miles of tunnels between Tonbridge and Battle had been built to a gauge that was markedly narrower than the national standard and meant that bespoke locomotives and rolling stock had to be provided.

Increasing patronage was causing train lengths to grow and steam traction was finding it more and more difficult to keep time. The Southern had built a class of 4-4-0s, the 'Schools', in 1930 specifically for passenger services between London and Hastings and these were the most powerful type permitted over the route.

The SR management realised that an interim arrangement would have to be found to satisfy public demand before electric traction could be applied, due to the Region's first electrification priority being the complete elimination of steam from Kent. It would therefore be 1963 at the earliest before electrification of the Tonbridge to Hastings route could be contemplated.

The Region decided to opt for a diesel-electric solution because this was judged to offer the desired improvement in the minimum amount of time. It is worth considering one option that was rejected, namely the provision of 'Hastings' gauge locomotives to haul the four eight-coach sets already under construction. The three prototype electric locomotives ordered by the Southern in the 1940s had been designed to fit the Hastings line when electrification eventually came. A variation of the SR's standard Type 3 was produced by BRCW to haul freight traffic over the route but this was eschewed for passenger duties, possibly because it offered only very limited extra power at the rail over steam. The new rolling stock was not only Hastings gauge in width, but only 56ft 11in long in order to be accommodated in the London termini from which the trains ran.

A study was undertaken to establish a traction requirement for a six-car set that could provide an end-to-end journey time of 90 minutes being demanded by customers, 11 minutes faster than steam. On the back of a contract the year before for diesel-electric locomotives, in 1946 EE had won a follow-on order for 19 complete diesel-electric trains for Egypt. These employed the EE model 4SRKT diesel and the SR had read reports that these had proved successful. Herein lay the solution for the Hastings line.

Within each six-car set, there would be a driving motor coach at each end with the EE engine rated at 500bhp driving a main generator. This would then supply power to two 250hp EE traction motors of the same type in general service within the SR's EMUs. This would provide about 800hp at the rail for each six-car set, achieve a large degree of standardisation with equipment already in use or planned on the Region, and offer a performance characteristic not too dissimilar to that of a standard four-car EMU up to the planned 75mph maximum speed.

A check was made to be certain that the planned power-to-weight ratio would be sufficient. Over the Crowhurst to Tunbridge Wells stretch, the most arduous part of the route, an increase of 50% in installed power was judged to yield a reduction of just 1½ minutes on the new projected timing of 29 minutes.

The intention was to have seven six-car sets in traffic (one as a maintenance spare) by the summer 1957 timetable and these would be diagrammed on the principal business services. This could be achieved by modification of the existing 32 hauled coaches already sanctioned in order to form five trains and by the building of a further two sets. Authorisation for the 'Hastings' DMUs was given on 24 March 1955 and a further 16 sets came later to enable steam passenger working to be eliminated. Construction of all the vehicles was at Eastleigh Works; however, the last batch employed the BR Standard Mark 1 carriage underframe, measuring 63ft 5in.

W. J. A. Sykes, the SR's CM&EE, read a paper about the Hastings DMUs to the Institution of Locomotive Engineers in 1960. It was customary for a senior member of the Institution to reply and propose a vote of thanks. In this instance, the reply was delivered by S. B .Warder, the CEE within the British Railways Central Staff ,and it is interesting to refer to some of his remarks because of the insight these offer into behind-the-scenes debate, and hence not always minuted in the official papers:

> A point not brought out by Sykes was the fact that the BTC had only agreed to the proposal after a process of presentation and representation of the most insistent supporting arguments. At the time when the proposition was put forward, there seemed to be only the diesel mechanical type of multiple-unit. No one had ever

really thought of a unit using an engine above the floor that was of this power. He well remembered coming back from the USA in 1954 when the proposition was first being discussed. At times the opposition had been quite violent. No one would believe that 500hp was enough. It had taken much persuasion and time before anyone would attempt it.

The subsequent upgrading of the engine from 500 to 600hp was, he would suggest, nothing to do with the case. It had been developed for special application in Hampshire. It was gratifying to hear that the operating and maintenance costs of these units compared so favourably with their diesel mechanical counterparts.

The Works Committee minutes for its meeting on 23 November 1955, when the Hasting DMU proposal was discussed, included comments from General Staff Advisors who queried whether reliable trainsets could be produced to the 1957 deadline. Clearly discord continued to the wire but Commission authority came shortly thereafter.

For whatever reason, no obvious thought was given to external styling. Contrary to the ethos of modernisation, the use of a 1951-pattern carriage did not compare well with the airy interior environment being provided in the mechanical-drive DMUs being built for the other Regions. Externally, a slab front and the slab sides demanded to fit the Hastings loading gauge brought an unfavourable public reaction, not helped by the use of unlined BR green livery.

The first full-scale demonstration run with a six-coach 'Hastings' unit took place from Eastleigh Works on 25 February 1957, with a 120-minute schedule over the 111½ miles between Waterloo and Bournemouth West. Service operation began on 6 May 1957 with 10 units, after a fire at Cannon Street signalbox put the station out of bounds to locomotives. Unusually for a modernisation project, sufficient sets were available ahead of schedule to permit this! The full service with 23 six-coach units commenced on 9 June 1958.

During the 1950s the SR had a significant number of branch and minor cross-country lines in Hampshire and Sussex. With a view to cost reduction, plans were drawn up more or less concurrent with the Hastings scheme for the building of 18 two-car versions of the 'Hastings' DMUs. These were for services linking Portsmouth with Salisbury, Southampton and Andover, and from Southampton and Alton and Winchester, and were to replace 20 steam locomotives and trainsets.

A recast timetable was introduced offering extra, regular-interval services and the 18 DMUs were diagrammed for a combined daily passenger train mileage of 6,058, which compared to 2,587 for steam. This demonstrates the operating efficiency gains that diesel traction made possible.

Later orders were for three-car formations, whilst trailer vehicles were added to the existing two-car batch because of the extra patronage they had engendered. Engine modifications brought an uplift in power to 600bhp but otherwise the powertrain was identical to the 'Hastings' DMUs.

The DMU building programme

With such a large programme, it was inevitable that there would be some twists and turns with DMU procurement as the years passed. In March 1958 the Commission returned to the subject in order to revise individual authorities, but excluding the SR's plans, covering the period from 1954 to 1958. The key issues must have seemed wearisome: revision of individual authorities in order to provide for increased costs, alterations in types of vehicles and changes in Regional requirements. Vehicle quantities were to be reduced by three but costs were to rise by nearly £2½ million to virtually £36 million for 2,556 vehicles.

Understandably this state of affairs did not pass without comment! It is clear that Commission Members were unhappy at the proliferation of designs and engine types. They wanted to see standardisation on a satisfactory minimum number of types which would provide an efficient service over the variety of operating conditions in the Regions. Design improvements were, though, considered desirable in certain aspects, one being ride quality.

Finally, Members accepted the recommendation of the Works Committee for an additional 627 vehicles under the 1959 building programme.

Also in 1958, the BTC was really up against it financially for reasons that will be dealt with in a later chapter. The focus on loss-making passenger services has been referred to already but the ScR wanted to avoid any withdrawals and for this reason was the keenest of all the Regions to pursue the railbus experiment. Naturally the Commission was aware that it did not make sense to run its own rail and bus operations in direct competition when one or the other, or even both, might be loss-making.

Investigations into this issue were clearly under way by the Commission meeting on 26 June because the Scottish Area Board chairman addressed the meeting. He said that his Board was experiencing difficulty in reaching a conclusion at that time regarding the benefits accruing to the Commission of the operation of DMUs or passenger road services over similar routes. Chairman Robertson batted the ball back by suggesting collaboration between the Scottish Area Board and the BTC's Scottish Omnibus Group, referral of the matter to the BTC's Railway Sub-Commission and Road Sub-Commission, and for the Area Board to assume the role of overseer on behalf of the Commission itself.

Nevertheless, steam replacement had by now become a headlong dash in order to save money and by 1961 there were some 4,000 DMU vehicles of all types in traffic. Within a few years a quarter of these had gone because the lines they served no longer carried passenger traffic. Capital assets, funded by loans from the Treasury, with an anticipated life of between 20 to 25 years had been written off in less than 10 years, a chronic waste. The Derby Lightweights, the progenitors of the standard DMU, were culled first.

Chapter 7

Electrification

AC or DC?

Within the Modernisation Plan £120 million had been allocated to main line electrification and £65 million to new and already authorised, but not yet announced, suburban schemes. It was therefore no surprise that the May 1955 announcement of modernisation schemes detailed work that ranged from planning to civil engineering on many of the electrification projects, including the lines in Essex, Kent and the West Coast route.

There was disappointment in some quarters at the apparent slow progress with these projects. Part of the reason was that Langdale Train's Technical Committee was wrestling with whether to continue with the 1932 Weir Committee overhead line supply standard of 1,500V DC, endorsed by the 1951 Railway Electrification Committee, or to emulate developments in France, where the Valenciennes to Thionville route had been wired at 25kV AC.

The topic was first considered on 11 March 1954 when SNCF progress was discussed and it was decided to carry out a technical and engineering appraisal for a typical main line. On 13 May both the ER and LMR were selected for a cost comparison between 25kV and 1,500V DC and it was felt that more experimental rolling stock was required.

In fact the implications of 50 cycles AC power supply had been set out in a report to the Technical Committee dated 10 September 1954 and this had been followed up in January 1955 by a memo signed jointly by S. B. Warder, the Chief Electrical Engineer on the BR Central Staff, and the LMR's Regional Manager. Investigations were to continue into several technical issues and French Railways consulted because of the significant progress being made by the latter in this field.

Warder continued evaluating options and he reported to the Technical Committee on 29 September 1955. The contents took account of practice on the Continent where DC electrification was much more extensive and where there was no logic in changing existing equipment until it became life-expired. However, countries such as Portugal and Turkey that had commenced new schemes had opted for 50 cycles (Hertz) AC, even though the former already had one route that had been electrified at 1,500V DC in 1924.

Warder started by arguing that times had moved on from the factors that decided the 1951 Committee to continue to recommend 1,500V DC. His decision to recommend AC overhead line supply was now the practice on the Continent for new schemes. When it came to traction, however, technology had not advanced sufficiently for the use of AC traction motors. In any event, DC motors had evolved to the point where they were relatively lightweight and very rugged, with a traction characteristic that suited rail applications very well.

Warder drew extensively on French experience with both types of electrification. There, a 78-ton locomotive had managed to restart a 2,400-ton train on a 1 in 100 gradient, whilst two other locomotives had achieved a world-record speed of 200mph, all using DC motors. For routine service, French Railways permitted a 970-ton load limit to its DC electrics and 1,400 tons to equivalent AC ones.

The main advantages of a 25kV AC supply were lighter overhead equipment and lower cost. This was because the copper conductor wire would be 50% smaller than for 1,500V DC, which was therefore lighter and so did not need such heavy-duty support equipment. These factors also cut costs. Warder estimated that an AC locomotive would cost 10% less than its DC equivalent.

A 1,500V DC system needed a large number of substations to counter voltage drop (where voltage drops the further away the collection point is from the substation); for example, on the Manchester, Sheffield and Wath system the interval was every 6.2 miles. By contrast, in France the higher-voltage 3kV DC lines achieved an interval of 20 miles. It wasn't possible to have individual supply from the national grid for each substation, and this brought the need for a railway-owned substation network. Comparing the two systems, the distance between Central Electricity Authority substations and railway-owned switching stations would be 17 miles for DC versus 250 miles for AC.

Locomotive control was more economical with AC because power was tapped from the locomotive transformer at pre-set points. With DC supply, control was achieved by having resistances connected in series with the traction motors. Only when all the resistances had been cut out was the highest economy in running achieved. Driver control was judged by footplate crew to be easier for AC traction.

Counterbalancing these factors, the much higher voltage required significantly larger clearances under overhead structures (bridges, tunnels and station canopies) and rebuilding these therefore added to the cost. To minimise this, Warder put forward the option of a dual-voltage arrangement, where 25kV would be used generally, but with 6.25kV (one quarter of 25kV) being used in, say, the London inner suburbs in order to avoid rebuilding structures.

Interference with telecommunications and colour-light signalling was also an issue that, unexpectedly, was found in some places to require complete replacement of existing colour-light equipment.

In advance of Warder's report, cost estimates for the proposed West Coast scheme out of Euston had been drawn up based on both AC and DC overhead supply. A figure of £118 million represented a saving of £6 million for the former.

Interestingly, for the WCML, freight train load limits for a single locomotive were estimated to be 900 tons for DC but 1,250 tons for AC. A maximum axleload of 20 tons and maximum tractive effort of 60,000lb were laid down and the power output needed for express passenger work was predicted to be around 3,500hp. It was estimated that for services between Euston, Birmingham, Liverpool and Manchester a total of 150 passenger and 510 mixed-traffic AC electrics would be needed at a total cost of £38,280,000, whereas for a DC system the number of mixed-traffic machines was given as 570 but each locomotive cost less and so the overall figure was £36,360,000. More DC machines were needed to handle the maximum anticipated trailing loads.

In conclusion, Warder favoured AC supply because of its superiority in the areas of power supply, fixed equipment and rolling stock.

The Technical Committee accepted Warder's report and, together with that containing cost estimates for the WCML, it was reviewed by the BTC on 19 October. Despite this consideration, in fine bureaucratic style the Commission deferred a final decision until the chairmen of the Area Boards and their Regional Managers had been consulted! In principle, however, a switch to 50 cycles AC was approved, except for the SR, and the Technical Committee was asked to investigate the implications for converting the ER London suburban schemes already authorised at 1,500V DC.

With Area Board chairmen and Regional Managers present, on the 27th the Commission returned to the topic. Referring to the proposed exclusion of the whole of the SR from the 50 cycle AC system, Sir Philip Warter (the SR Area Board chairman) wanted the option left open for its adoption, if practicable, for this system on the Region's western section. For this reason he preferred the exception to be confined to the east and central sections of the SR.

The national standard for main line electrification was a Government-directed matter and the Commission informed the MoT of its intention to change to 25kV as the new standard. A note dated 3 December 1955 in the MoT files observes that the creation of the BTC had removed the need for Government to opine on this matter. On 31 May 1956 the Commission recorded the Minister's affirmation of the decision.

Returning to the ER schemes already in progress, on 17 November the Commission considered a submission by the Technical Committee of the 10th that 50 cycles AC be adopted for all electrified lines in the eastern section of the ER. Eminent outside consulting engineers were satisfied with the advantage of 50 cycles AC and adoption would not delay opening to electric traction of any of the ER's lines to be electrified. This recommendation was accepted in the knowledge that the lines from Shenfield to Chelmsford and Southend would be electrified on the 1,500V DC system, prior to their eventual conversion.

West Coast electrification
Returning to the Commission's meeting on 27 October 1955, Barker argued that the whole scheme for LMR electrification be approved, not just the Crewe to Manchester section. The Central Staff's rationale was that this short section would serve as a proving ground for the system but Barker's argument was that the system was proven, albeit overseas at 25kV, and it was only the equipment that needed proving. Yet again, his advice was ignored and approval was given for planning work only to commence on the rest of the route south of Crewe. Five years down the line, approval to electrify south of Crewe was nearly withheld by the MoT, a situation that wouldn't have arisen if the BTC had sanctioned and started on the entire scheme in line with Barker's contention. Barker's proposal to try out new equipment before mass introduction should also have been heeded because traction components bought *en bloc* for the Glasgow and Great Eastern schemes gave trouble.

At the Commission's meeting on 15 March 1956 the go-ahead was given to the first phase of the Crewe to Manchester scheme between Wilmslow and Slade Lane Junction (the Styal line). Over a year passed before the BTC sanctioned further work on 25 April 1957 for the remainder of the Crewe to Manchester scheme and for preliminary work on the Crewe-Liverpool section.

At the same time, Commission Members wanted HQ officers to consult with Regional colleagues to see whether a broad assessment of the financial impact of electrification of Crewe to Manchester could be made 'without a disproportionate occupation of time'. The Deputy Chairman asked if the proposed expenditure was in line with the figure included for this work in the Plan, and was told costs of this particular section were higher proportionately than were expected for the country as a whole. This was because it was a pioneer scheme and included certain expenditure which would not be repeated. Also apart from this, the cost of electrification had risen in keeping with the general increase in prices in recent years.

Pre-Modernisation developments

Above: Pre-nationalisation locomotive designs continued to be built into the 1950s. Former GWR 'Castle' class No 7010 *Avondale Castle* was built in June 1948 and survived until 1964. This picture finds it at Old Oak Common on 25 July 1962. *P. J. Lynch*

Below: The Railway Executive opted for steam power for main line services as a stop-gap until funds were available for electrification. No 70000 *Britannia* was the first of its class and the first of a new range of BR locomotives designed by R. A. Riddles and is captured in a run-down state near Kenton, south of Harrow, on the West Coast line with a down express freight on 20 April 1963. Built in 1951, it succumbed in 1966. *Dr D. P. Williams*

Above: By its demise in 1953, the Railway Executive had a small number of modern traction units, which it eschewed in preference to steam. No 10203 actually emerged in 1954 as an updated version of a Southern Railway design and was the basis for the English Electric Pilot Scheme Type 4. *Ian Allan Library*

Below: The Great Western Railway built over 30 diesel railcars during the 1930s for a range of services and these proved to be a success. Despite this, it took an internal report in 1951 before the Railway Executive showed interest in such traction for branch services. On 4 November 1961 a GWR railcar forms the 1.56pm to Worcester at Bromyard, the service beyond here having gone a decade earlier. *E. Wilmshurst*

Above: Following from the 1951 report, the Railway Executive commissioned a study of services suitable for conversion to railcar operation. One of the first routes to be dealt with was between Penrith and Workington. Typical gloomy Lake District weather sets the scene at Bassenthwaite Lake in August 1962 as a two-car Derby Lightweight set heads a westbound service. *R. L. Sewell*

Below: The standard British Railways shunter (Class 08) was based on a design by the LMSR in the 1930s and fitted with an English Electric powertrain. No 3018 shunts north of Carlisle. *EE*

Above: Prior to the Modernisation Plan, the UK electrification standard was 1,500V DC overhead supply. The Manchester, Sheffield and Wath route was completed in 1954 to this pattern and Class 76 No 26023 brings a loaded coal train from Yorkshire through east Manchester. *AEI*

Modern diesel designs

Below: Private contractors were given some freedom with styling and did a far superior job than contemporary railway workshops. Metropolitan-Cammell is acknowledged as producing one of the best-styled and most durable designs of DMU and this is evident in this view of an Ipswich-bound service at a beautifully-maintained station. *Ian Allan Library*

Above: Still on Great Eastern lines but this time a suburban service, the Cravens DMU at Liverpool Street on 30 August 1958 appears to be newly-delivered. Front-end speed whiskers were favoured by builders but detested by industrial designers and disappeared under the influence of the latter. *Brian Haresnape*

Below: Proof of railway works' dreadful aesthetics can be found in Class 302, which also appeared in 1958 and came from York and Doncaster for the newly-electrified Fenchurch Street to Shoeburyness line. On 5 September 1966 the 11.35 down is seen at Leigh on Sea. *G. R. Mortimer*

Above: Just one year separates the introduction of Classes 302 and 303 (seen here) but their appearance suggests a completely different era. The latter was built for Glasgow suburban electrification by Pressed Steel with Design Panel assistance. *Ian Allan Library*

Above: Railbuses were viewed by some, but not all, Regions as a low-cost saviour of rural branches but they weren't. On 2 May 1959 a railbus waits at Kemble, Gloucestershire, for its next run to Tetbury. *C. J. Gammell*

Below: The '4CEP' EMUs were part of the Kent Coast electrification scheme authorised in the 1955 Plan. Not quite as austere-looking as other railway-designed stock, they were far from modern in a number of respects. Two sets, unit 7139 leading, are seen near Meopham with an unidentified two-car set at the rear. *BR*

Above: By the time the railways built Class 309 for the Clacton electrification, the Design Panel had worked some magic on styling when compared to the earlier 4CEPs. A down working threads through Stratford en route from Liverpool Street. *Ian Allan Library*

Below: Staying with rolling stock design, the light, airy ambience of the Class 310 suburban EMUs built for duties out of Euston is evident here, where at least one passenger is a Harrow resident. *BR*

Locomotive styling

Above: One of the worst examples of poor styling was Derby's Class 24, of which an external consultant, who was asked to advise on a new livery, commented that you couldn't make a silk purse out of a pig. On 22 April 1960 Class 24 No D5007 approaches Bearsted with a Maidstone East to Ashford stopper. *David N. Clough*

Below: Among the Pilot Scheme classes, the BRCW Type 2 (Class 26) was acknowledged as one of the best for appearance. In July 1959 No D5314 sits in the stabling siding at King's Cross York Road, whilst 68930 emerges from Gasworks Tunnel on a transfer freight bound for the SR via the widened lines. *Brian Haresnape*

Above: Unlike French and German railways, British Railways did not impose a house style and a hotch-potch was the result, as exemplified by this view at Swindon on 24 January 1965. From left to right are examples of Classes 52, 37, 47 and 35. *D. H. Cape*

Below: The English Electric 'house style' of the 1950s for its twin-cab diesels was to have a front nose end. Whilst the Class 40 on the right might be described as purposeful, the Design Panel influence on the Class 55 on the left is evident, albeit that the Panel didn't want a nose at all!

Above: Unrelieved standard Locomotive Green produced an unimpressive locomotive, far from the 'stimulating' appearance sought by a BTC Member. Horizontal light grey lining was used to break up the bulk of the body sides and its usefulness is brought out here in Derby's Class 46 No D139. *BR*

Below: A range of designs of its own manufacture were lined up by English Electric at its Vulcan Works, with Class 73 No E6009, Class 86 No E3193, Class 20 No D8128 and the final Class 37 No D6608, with an industrial shunter alongside. *EE*

Above: The standard Type 4, Class 47, was used to launch a new corporate livery and emblem. *Deighton Wilkes & Co official photo*

Above right: The interior of the new Euston station. *BR 2*

Right: The interior of the new box at Newcastle Central in 1959 finds the signalmen 'suited and booted' and provided with a carpet to cushion their feet. Note the dais for the person-in-charge, who is seated, naturally! *BR*

Above: The new marshalling yard at Perth in 1962. *BR*

Below: Some new marshalling yards were built on the 'hump' principle, where wagons were pushed over a hump from where they coasted by gravity, slowed by trackside retarders, before being routed into the required siding. *EE*

Above: London's new international freight terminal at Stratford. *British Lighting Industries Ltd*

Below: Goods inwards at the new Stockton-on-Tees freight depot. From here the goods will be loaded onto a road vehicle and delivered, whereas a road haulier would simply transport door-to-door without intermediate handling. How did railway managers believe they could operate this at a profit? *BR*

Left: Railfreight – the way forward. The container terminal at Longsight, Manchester. *BR*

Below: Modern traction maintenance portrayed here in 1957 by Crewe depot, with brand-new examples of a Class 20 and Class 104 DMUs. *BR*

Above right: Modernisation in progress at Preston on 23 May 1968. Class 25 No D7576 heads the Manchester portion of the combined service from Glasgow to Liverpool Exchange whilst an '08' hauling a trip working waits for a down freight to pass. In addition to the traction, the roof of the goods depot has been rebuilt but it will be 1972 before the semaphore signals are replaced. *Derek Cross*

Types of express services

Above: The BTC decided there would be three types of express passenger trains and the premier category was the Pullman. On 30 August 1962 a 'Blue Pullman' with power cars Nos 60097 and 60096 passes Solihull en route between Birmingham and Paddington. *A. F. Porter*

Above: As owners of the Pullman brand, BR tried to capitalise on its investment. Twenty-nine hauled coaches to the latest Mark 2 design but also air-conditioned were built in 1964 for use between Euston, Liverpool and Manchester and were the last dedicated Pullman vehicles. Class 86 No E3141 poses for an official photo. *BR*

Below: Regions could also operate 'special' expresses that did not conform to the normal pattern of services. There were several of these on the East Coast line, such as the 'Flying Scotsman' pictured here on 6 June 1962 behind Class 55 No D9016 (later named *Gordon Highlander*). Whilst the caption says the train is heading north, the train reporting number suggests otherwise! *BR*

Above: The WR 'Bristolian' had a long tradition into the 1960s as a fast non-stop working in the up direction. By 25 June 1971 it was still regarded as a prestige train but its traction and rolling stock were indistinguishable from other workings on the route. Class 47 No 1606 accelerates the up train past a full yard at St Annes, Bristol. *P. J. Fowler*

Above: Built specially for a new inter-city service linking Hull and Liverpool, the Class 124 'Trans-Pennine' DMUs had the highest power-to-weight ratio of any DMU and a unique griddle car offering hot food. Saddleworth Viaduct is being crossed by a westbound train coasting down to Stalybridge on 17 March 1974. *David N. Clough*

Below: The ordinary express of the Modernisation Plan was powered by a Type 4 diesel (or two Type 2s in Scotland) or possibly a Type 5 on the East Coast. Save for the Pullmans, the electrics on the West Coast ran to a standard pattern. Class 40 No D310 heads a diverted Euston to Blackpool express past Sandersons Sidings, Worsley, west of Manchester, on 28 August 1961. *J. R. Carter*

Above: The standard 2,750hp Type 4 was not always sufficiently powerful to haul expresses at average speeds of 75mph. Class 55s of 3,300hp were used on the East Coast, whilst from 1970 double-heading was resorted to between Crewe and Glasgow. Nos 50008 and 50038 approach Preston on 6 April 1974 with the 13.10 Glasgow Central to Euston. *David N. Clough*

Modern freight workings

Below: Surely a staged photo, with a lorry conveying a container for rail transport passing a container working on the West Coast line. *BR*

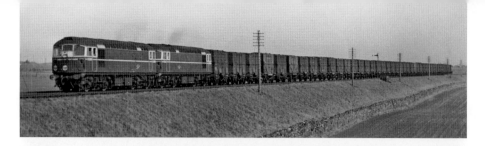

Top: Just south of Aberdeen in May 1961 a block meat train heads for King's Cross behind two Class 26 diesels. *BR*

Above: Unbraked mineral wagons were still running well into the 1980s and were marshalled behind braked vehicles in a partially-fitted train such as this Severn Tunnel Junction to Acton Yard merchandise service. Class 43 No 839 *Relentless* is the motive power on 25 June 1970. *David N. Clough*

Below: After a stand-off for several years, BR and the NCB agreed to the mgr method of operation of coal trains. On 14 April 1991 Class 20 Nos 20055 and 20028 tow HAA wagons through Parkside Colliery's loading bunker near Newton le Willows, Merseyside. *David N. Clough*

Above: Down to 1963 professional railway managers failed to win a fair share of the burgeoning oil traffic and it was Dr Beeching's team which then redressed the situation. On 14 January 1985 Class 40 No 40194 stands in the former Manchester Exchange with a train bound for Stanlow oil refinery. *David N. Clough*

Below: The block cement service between Cliffe (Kent) and Uddingston (Lanarkshire) was another type of cargo that grew in the 1960s and of which the railways won a good share. An unmodernised scene at Hitchin in July 1974, with a varied array of wagons in the yard, frames Class 47 No 1971 as it heads north. *G. F. Burton*

Above: Company-branded trains became common during the 1960s, the Ford Motor Company being one of the first. Class 85 No E3101 heads south along the West Coast line for Dagenham. *Gordon Whiting official photo*

Below: Railway modernisation is continual. This is a Research Department prototype of the dual-supply Class 313 sets for the Great Northern inner suburban electrification in 1976. *BR*

In addition to the rebuilding of Manchester London Road station, then renamed Piccadilly, as well as those at Crewe and Stockport, 82 of the 92 overbridges along the route required major work to obtain the necessary clearance for 25kV. Three short tunnels at Stockport were opened out completely for the same reason and these civil engineering works go some way to explaining the cost over-run on the project.

The Electric Pilot Scheme

On 25 April 1956 the Works Committee gave approval for the issuing of tenders to contractors for 40 mixed-traffic and 20 express passenger complete locomotives and for the equipments for 20 mixed-traffic and 20 passenger locomotives to be built in BR shops. Brief price and performance data was received from a number of contractors but these proved incapable of comparison and further work had to be carried out to permit proper assessment.

Lessons seem to have been learned from the diesel Pilot Scheme, where contractors were given largely a free hand in design and a consequential wide diversity in some aspects where standardisation would have been desirable. What the Works Committee did now was to specify a Bo-Bo wheel arrangement and 20-ton maximum axle load, together with a standard arrangement of driving controls. Pantographs (two per locomotive) and circuit breakers were also to be of a single type across all the classes.

Another stipulation added by the Works Committee was that the traction motors must be bogie-mounted and not axle-hung. All of the diesel-electric pilots had the latter arrangement but this caused considerably greater track damage because of the much greater unsprung mass. This was an issue that grew in significance in direct proportion to train speed and was thus highly pertinent for the proposed West Coast route, where the expresses would be sustaining high speed.

There were, effectively, two patentees of bogie-mounted motor drives, Brown-Boveri of Switzerland and Alsthom of France. Both had British licensees but the former stipulated that the initial equipment had to be made in Switzerland and this added significantly to cost. For tender evaluation, the Works Committee based the price comparisons on the use of axle-hung motors.

The performance characteristics laid down for the electrics was such that operating in multiple was not envisaged and this provided a saving. Train heating was initially to be dealt with by the use of heating vans behind the locomotive until sufficient carriages with ETH had been put into traffic. Then the locomotive would provide a supply up to 320kW at 800A.

A meeting of the Technical Committee on 13 May 1958 received a report on the difficulties caused by fine snow to the United States Pennsylvania Railroad's electric locomotives. Warder confirmed the design policy of British Railways was to streamline air passages in order to avoid pockets and corners.

With sanction for electrification of the Crewe to Liverpool route having been given, the LMR had reassessed its traction requirements for this and the Manchester line. Now it was proposed to have 75 mixed-traffic examples and a performance specification for the Pilot Scheme orders reassessed. This was for a capability to haul a 475-ton passenger train at up to 100mph and a 950-ton freight at 55mph; these were to be designated mixed-traffic Type A.

Electrification south of Crewe was speculated as possibly needing a mixed-traffic Type B design, with a 75mph top speed but capable of handling 1,250-ton trains at 55mph. The different performance characteristic was to be achieved by the relatively straightforward expedient of using a different traction motor gear ratio. As part of the standardisation, where a contractor was to supply equipment for both Types A and B, the traction motors were to be of a single design.

It was not until 12 January 1957 that proposals could be put to the Works Committee for 100 locomotives. Dealing first with a bid from Brown-Boveri comprising a 61-ton locomotive, this was judged to be inadequate for the specified duties and a second bid of a larger model was highly uncompetitive when import duty was added.

This left four British electrical manufacturers, all of which quoted for both the supply of electrical equipment and also complete locomotives. In both cases, British Thomson Houston (BTH) offered the lowest prices, although the highest tender (from Metrovick) was only 11% higher. It was felt desirable to order from all four manufacturers, however, in order to assess the full range of equipment available, which included the patented flexible drives of Brown-Boveri and Alsthom.

On the 24th the Works Committee's recommendations were discussed by the Commission. Of course Pope and Train, who led the Works Committee, were also full-time Commission Members. After discussion, it was decided to vary the orders by reallocating five locomotives to be built by EE to BTH/BRCW instead. Whilst the Works Committee's view was to spread orders between several manufacturers in order to assess different equipment, the Commission made it clear that, ultimately, a standard locomotive was the intention.

The cost of the orders was £6 million. Of note was that the 80 Type As would be allocated to the LMR but no decision had been taken on the allocation of the 20 Type Bs.

Table 6 sets out the breakdown of the orders. Whilst those from contractors were part of the 1959 Building Programme, those from Doncaster were put into 1960.

The traction motors to be supplied by both BTH and Metrovick were to be identical, reflecting the relationship between these companies. In fact both were part of Associated Electrical Industries (AEI) and the decision was taken by the latter at the end of 1959 to merge the separate identities of BTH and Metrovick under the AEI brand.

Four locomotives were required for testing and training by June 1958 and the remaining 38 required by the LMR for the full Crewe to Manchester route by June 1959. Even at the date of the memo, it was accepted that the initial

Table 6 Electric Pilot Scheme orders

	Drive	Type A	Type B
BTH (BRCW)	BB	20	5
Metrovick (Beyer Peacock)	BB	5	5
EE (Vulcan Foundry)	A	10	5
General Electric Co (NBL)	A	5	5
BTH (Doncaster Works)	BB	40	

BB = Brown Boveri, A = Alsthom
The names in brackets are the builders of the mechanical parts.

Table 7 Electric locomotive details

Contractor	Class	TOPS Class	Type	Rating (hp)	Numbering	Built
BTH/BRCW	AL1	81	A	3,388	E3001-23	11/59-2/62
			B		E3301-2	8/61*
Metrovick	AL2	82	A	3,388	E3046-55	5/60-8/61
EE	AL3	83	A	2,960	E3024-35	7/60-7/61
			B		E3303-5	2/61-6/62**
GEC	AL4	84	A	3,000	E3036-45	3/60-3/61
BTH/BR	AL5	85	A	3,388	E3056-95	6/61-12/64***

* – E3302 has no official record until 1964. E3301 was built in 1961 and E3023 in February 1962.
** – E3305 seems never to have carried this number and may actually have been built as a Type A and numbered No E3100.
*** – The last few examples appear to have been put into store after completion for up to a year before being taken into stock on the date shown.
After trials, it was decided to abandon Type B in 1962 and these examples were converted to Type A.

deliveries would not arrive until the end of 1958. In the event, producing a design with a maximum axle load of 20 tons proved very challenging and deliveries from all the contractors were late.

Locomotive commissioning and crew training was carried out on the Styal loop. It was now clear that deliveries of locomotives was behind the electrification plan and the Operating Department wanted to get staff training under way as quickly as possible. Chapter 2 referred to the Metrovick gas turbine prototype No 18100 which had been built for the WR but put to store in 1953 because it was wholly uneconomic on fuel. A decision was taken in December 1957 to convert No 18100 into Britain's first 25kV AC locomotive to serve as a test-bed and for crew training. Metrovick had been the main contractor for its construction and was contracted to carry out the conversion. This was done at the Stockton-on-Tees works of the Metrovick/Beyer Peacock joint venture and the location of the construction of the diesel Pilot Scheme order to Metrovick for the Crossley Type 2 'D5700' series.

The resultant conversion was completed quickly and No 18100 reappeared in October 1958, with subsequent renumbering, initially as E1000 and then E2001. In 1961 No E2001 spent a spell on the electrified Glasgow suburban network before moving back to the LMR, where it was predominantly in store but with limited use at Rugby for static training. It was withdrawn from there in April 1968.

Suburban and stopping services were to be diagrammed for four-car EMUs – Class AM4. These were built at the railway's works at Wolverton and a first batch of 15 was delivered in April 1960, followed by a further 21 for Crewe to Liverpool in 1961 and finally nine in 1962 for use south of Crewe to Birmingham and Rugby. Traction equipment was of BTH manufacture and four traction motors gave a combined power of 828hp, whilst 75mph was the maximum speed.

Maintenance for the motive power was to be provided by three depots. One was within the Manchester Longsight complex, whilst new depots were built at Crewe (close to the works) and at Allerton in Liverpool.

The Crewe to Manchester services were inaugurated on 12 September 1960, No E3040 taking the first train. Crewe to Liverpool Lime Street followed on 1 January 1962. A report in December 1960 to the Technical Committee on locomotive performance to date said that the EE and GEC examples had been practically trouble-free. More extensive alterations had been necessary on the AEI Rugby version and, when completed, there was no reason to suppose the result would not be entirely satisfactory.

SR electrification

In response to the need to provide and operate an intensive rush-hour service, the Southern Railway had gradually electrified a number of inner-suburban routes, primarily in what was the Central Division. The system used was a 750V DC third-rail current supply and, by the time of the Modernisation Plan, this was regarded as too extensive to convert to the new standard 25kV AC overhead supply arrangement. This policy disappointed the Southern Area Board chairman who, nevertheless, hoped the AC format could be used for the Region's Western Division.

By 1955 the SR had developed standard designs of EMUs that offered performances that were uniform, consistent and provided fast acceleration. For example, a Class 4EPB set offered 7.4hp/ton, whilst a new design of three-car DMU fitted with 150bhp engines had a power-to-weight ratio of about 6.5hp/ton. For locomotive-hauled trainsets, a similar power-to-weight ratio for a Class 7 steam locomotive or a 2,000hp diesel would see a consist of just two coaches!

Within the Modernisation Plan, the major scheme of electrification proposed for the SR was routes in Kent to the coast. At the Commission's meeting on 16 February 1956 the Area Board chairman presented proposals and these were approved in principle. He expressed disappointment again that the third-rail system would be used because he would have preferred 25kV AC. The meeting asked the General Staff if a good allocation of Type 2 diesel-electrics from the Pilot Scheme could be tried out on the SR.

The scheme was divided into two phases, the first comprising routes between:

Gillingham–Faversham–Ramsgate
Sittingbourne–Sheerness
Sittingbourne (Western Junction–Middle Junction)–Faversham–Dover Marine
Stewarts Lane area

Phase 2 covered:
Sevenoaks–Ashford–Dover–Ramsgate
Maidstone East–Ashford–Canterbury West–Minster junctions
Paddock Wood–Maidstone West
Folkestone Harbour branch

Tonbridge to Hastings was excluded because there was insufficient time and resource to re-gauge the route to the British Railways standard.

Seventy-eight stations were improved, including the extension of platforms to take 12 cars (which was happening elsewhere on the SR) and the replacement of gas with electric lighting. Curves were realigned, junctions re-laid, track arrangements altered and four lines provided instead of two.

The railway infrastructure was upgraded, including the installation of colour-light signalling between Victoria and Ramsgate via Chatham and also between Hither Green and Dover via Tonbridge. Phase 1 was commissioned in 1959 and saw 31 manual boxes replaced by power boxes at Factory Junction, Shepherds Lane, Herne Hill, Beckenham Junction, Shortlands Junction, Chislehurst Junction, Rochester Bridge Junction, Rainham, Sittingbourne and Faversham. Phase 2 included new power boxes at Hither Green, Orpington, Sevenoaks, Tonbridge, Ashford and Folkestone Junction and commissioning began in 1962, with 41 manual boxes closing.

Note the long interval between the commissioning dates for the two phases. Major resignalling schemes proved to be far more complex and demanding on resources than envisaged at the planning stage. This applied equally to the railways and the electrical supply industry. In some cases, additional technicians were brought in from abroad.

New traction maintenance depots were built at Stewarts Lane, London, Ashford, Chart Leacon and Ramsgate.

Motive power

A British Railways standard-pattern four-car corridor EMU designated 4CEP (later Class 411) was built in the railway's works at Eastleigh and was based on the prewar 4COR design for the Portsmouth electrification. Each set comprised two driving motor coaches and two trailer cars. Four 250hp EE traction motors were fitted in each set, retaining a uniform power-to-weight ratio with earlier EMUs that was vital for the operation of an intensive service at headways as tight as three minutes. Including those with a buffet car in place of one of the trailers (designated 4BEP), a total of 133 sets were built, with later orders being used elsewhere on the Region. Prototypes began to appear on the Central Division during 1956.

Whilst the above were intended for express services (CEP standing for corridor express passenger), a series of two-car 2HAP units (later Class 414) were built for semi-fast duties. Again, traction equipment came from EE and gave 500hp per set. In all 104 sets were built for both phases.

Ten motor luggage vans were also built to convey passengers' belongings and mail associated with the cross-Channel traffic. Each had two 250hp traction motors, with batteries and an auxiliary generator enabling operation off the third rail. Adding an unpowered vehicle to a 4CEP would have reduced its power-to-weight ratio and also made ascending the 1 in 30 Folkestone Harbour branch difficult.

The Southern had built three 1,470hp Co-Co electrics during the 1940s. Experience gained helped with the design of 13, later increased to 24, new 2,552hp Bo-Bo examples capable of 90mph for the Kent Coast scheme. These were required to match EMU performance on boat trains, as well as being capable of hauling a 900-ton freight train up a gradient of 1 in 100.

Built at Doncaster and numbered from E5000, these were taken into traffic during 1959 and 1960. Traction equipment was of EE manufacture and included an auxiliary generator, which was driven by a flywheel, to cope with gaps in the third rail, and dubbed a booster. A pantograph was fitted to collect power from an overhead line supply in yards and sidings where it was too dangerous to lay the third rail. Designated Class HA, utilisation was on freight and heavy Continental traffic to Dover and Newhaven.

On 30 December 1957 the BTC Press Office announced the placing of an order with BRCW as main contractor for the construction of 45 1,550hp Bo-Bo diesels for Phase 1 of the SR Kent Coast modernisation. The press release referred to use on freight and inter-regional passenger services and delivery was required by September 1959. By then, the BTC had already authorised a further 20 examples, which the SR said were required for Phase 2, and it was noted that the first tranche had yet to be ordered! Due to a change in procedures within headquarters, a year was to elapse before the contract for the second series was let to BRCW.

This was the first order within the newly-created Type 3 power class. BRCW used the same mechanical parts it had designed for its Pilot Scheme order for 20 Type 2s, the D5300 series, but substituted an eight cylinder version of Sulzer's LDA28 diesel but still with electrical equipment of Crompton Parkinson manufacture. The SR's decision to require ETH enabled the steam generator fitted to the Type 2 to be omitted and so the larger engine could be accommodated in the same body shell. Maximum speed was to be 85mph, the limit then prevailing on the Region.

No D6500 was delivered on 17 December 1959, following closely on the heels of BRCW's last Type 2 of what became Class 26. In the meantime, and in line with the Commission's request, a tranche of Derby's Pilot Scheme Type 2s were allocated to the SR virtually from their emergence from works commencing in January 1959.

The origins of the so-called electro-diesel (ED) can be traced to a meeting of the Technical Committee on 13 December 1957, where the feasibility of modifying a standard motor coach to include a small diesel engine at one end for working on SR non-electrified lines was raised. Fast forward to the Committee's meeting on 15 May 1959 when it was proposed that prototype electric locomotives which incorporated a small diesel engine should be capable of being put into traffic by September 1961. This would then give the possibility of using these to replace Type 3 diesels on duties of limited power on the SR.

An order was placed with EE as main contractor, but with the mechanical parts to be manufactured at Eastleigh Works for six locomotives. With a continuous rating of 1,420hp (1,600hp for one hour), these were not as powerful as the 'HAs' but could work in multiple. An EE 6SRKT diesel with a one-hour rating of 600bhp and identical to that being used in the SR's DMUs was included within the body. Delivery of all six of Class JA came during 1962 and, proving to be successful, a further 43 were built at Vulcan Foundry, though with maximum speed raised from the 80mph of the prototypes to 90.

Electric traction took over on 15 June 1959 between London and Dover via Gillingham to both Ramsgate and Dover Marine (via Canterbury East), and from Sittingbourne over the Swale Bridge to Sheerness-on-Sea. The Motor Luggage Vans began operation in May and the 'HAs' took over the working of Continental Boat Trains from 8 June.

Phase 2 electric services began between London and Dover via Tonbridge, and between Paddock Wood and Maidstone West on 6 June 1961. With resignalling finally fully commissioned in 1962, the full electric service was introduced on 18 June. Services were planned on regular-interval timetables and trains from Victoria split at Gillingham to serve Ramsgate and Dover.

Glasgow suburban electrification Phase 1
Despite earlier foreboding about the cost and viability of the scheme, the recommendation of the Inglis Report for electrification of the Glasgow suburban network was sanctioned as part of the Modernisation Plan. Phase 1 was also variously known as the North Clyde and the Glasgow North Electric Suburban Line and was centred on the cross-city route through Queen Street Low Level. The lines electrified at 25kV AC encompassed Helensburgh Central to Airdrie, as well as the branches to Balloch Pier, Milngavie, Springburn and Bridgeton (Central), a total of some 52 route miles. The published cost of the scheme was £16 million.

As with the majority of similar schemes, track remodelling took place at some locations and new stations were added. Perhaps for the first time on British Railways, route branding was applied, possibly because this was the first project to start after the creation of the BTC Design Panel; more about the Panel will be said in a later chapter. A common theme between stations and rolling stock was the use of the former Caledonian Railway blue as part of the paint scheme. Overlapping 'V's in yellow and blue on a black background was the branding motif used.

Tunnel clearances in the central area were too restrictive for 25kV and so 6.25kV was adopted in this section. A maintenance depot for the new stock was built at Hyndland.

The 91 three-car trainsets had Metrovick electrics and the four traction motors per set were rated at 828hp continuously, geared for a 75mph maximum speed. Of these, 58 were for the North Clyde and the remainder for south of the river. The BTC minute of 9 May 1957 appertaining to the ordering of these EMUs is interesting. The Works Committee's recommendation that Pressed Steel Company of Linwood, near Paisley, Lanarkshire, be invited to tender for the design contract and for the construction of some of the vehicles was agreed but subject to the price tendered and for not more than 50% of the total requirement.

Pressure to allocate an order for motive power construction destined for a Scottish modernisation scheme to a Scottish contractor was to recur in future years. As was generally the case when orders were to be placed outside the railways' own works, the BTC minute added the rider that the announcement of the order should be most carefully handled; they couldn't upset the railway unions! In the event, Pressed Steel built the whole class.

Whilst 9ft was the standard width for rolling stock, the new EMUs were sanctioned to be an extra 3in wider. The ScR Regional Manager apparently insisted that the forward view for passengers behind the driver should be as panoramic as in an observation car. Design Panel influence in styling was also evident and the Electric Blue livery (as the colour was known) created a very striking impact and led to these Class AM3 EMUs being dubbed the 'Blue Trains'.

The North Clyde lines served both large urban conurbations and the full panoply of industrial installations from large shipbuilding to light engineering. A standard-pattern service, augmented during the rush hour, was implemented and the journey time from Helensburgh Central to Queen Street was cut from 64 minutes with steam to 51 with the new EMUs, and the number of trains increased from 24 to 37. Airdrie saw a much more dramatic boost in frequency, with 75 in place of 25 trains each day. Chairman Robertson inaugurated the new service on Saturday 5 November 1960 but the full timetable did not commence until Monday the 7th. One report claimed that patronage eventually grew to double that of the steam service.

Electrification progress

As BTC finances continued to worsen, on 31 January 1957 Robertson said loss-making had to be curtailed by the end of 1961. One plank towards achieving this was the on-time completion of the first round of modernisation projects and consequential elimination of steam. In addition to Crewe/Manchester/Liverpool and Phase 1 of both Kent Coast and Glasgow, also included were the Great Eastern routes (London to Tilbury/Southend/Enfield, Chingford/Hertford and Bishops Stortford). The three projects described above sought to bring out key aspects of modernisation that began to have general ubiquity.

Sadly, some technical issues affected the new AC rolling stock operating the Glasgow and Great Eastern services and those on the former had to be replaced by a cobbled-together steam and diesel operation for a year. These issues were discussed by the Technical Committee in December 1960, and it was noted that the BTH equipment in the Manchester EMUs had performed satisfactorily. Some Members on the ER, who had grown up with 1,500V DC, had viewed the decision in 1956 to switch to AC with some scepticism and now felt vindicated and some in the electrical industry supported them.

The French had spent four years testing 25kV equipment before 'going live' on a main line and this enabled review and reassessment of designs. British Railways approached AC electrification at breakneck speed and without any 'proving', save for the short, low-intensity Lancaster to Morecambe/Heysham route. The lack of equipment testing was aggravated by the decision to opt for dual voltage – 6.25kV as well as 25kV – in order to save money and time where clearances between structures and the live wire were tight. Issues arising from the switching between these voltages were not considered fully by manufacturers.

Another factor was that the height of the overhead wire could vary by as much as 6ft 5in between parts of the lower and higher voltage tracks. The pantograph had to cope with this wide variation. However, in certain locations when at full stretch (as it were), it could bounce against the conductor wire and so cause repeated breaks in connectivity. Again, the electrical equipment in the EMUs had not been designed to cope with this.

Of course, squadron production of AC locomotives was not followed, with the Pilot Scheme of orders to five manufacturers enabling differences in equipment design to be evaluated. Whilst some technical problems did arise, even though the mileages capable of being run between Crewe to Manchester and later Liverpool were insubstantial, sufficient was learned to shape decisions when the time came to order the next tranche of locomotives.

Chapter 8

A journey through design

This is an aspect of British Railways' fleet that receives scant attention but the official files, in the National Archives, provide a rich source of material. There are several strands to this topic: technical design, aesthetic design (styling) and livery. As regards technical design, much has been written elsewhere in this book concerning how these decisions were taken about locomotives and DMUs.

Styling

As regards styling, the Commission missed a trick when the Pilot Scheme contracts were awarded in not emulating French and German practice of electing for a 'house style'. Each manufacturer was given free rein, but with input from Ted Cox, the head of locomotive design within the Central Staff. The basic issue was that one design of mechanical parts capable of accommodating power equipment from different manufacturers was not produced for the diesel Pilot Scheme. Instead, manufacturers were given licence to produce a traction unit without BTC control. Lessons were learned from this and the five electric Pilot Scheme classes were built to Commission-dictated parameters and looked broadly similar, even though the various manufacturers were given freedom to use their own equipment.

External styling was given low priority by both the contractors and Derby Works and many of the diesel pilot classes suffered accordingly. Contractors often opposed proposals from the Commission and the external design consultants it appointed to advise, including technical factors such as the necessary positioning of internal equipment dictating the location of external grilles. Class 24 is a case in point. The Derby drawing office took no notice of recommendations made by the external consultant who had been appointed by the BTC Design Panel, and the result was something of an ugly duckling. In fact, in 1962, when the consultant was asked to advise on a change of livery, he replied that 'it was not possible to make a silk purse out of a pig'.

Keith Grand, the WR Regional Manager, took a close interest in the appearance of the Swindon-designed 'V200s' and the records show he had to approve every decision, trumping BR Central Staff views in this area.

Sitting over Grand was the Western Area Board and its chairman, Reginald Hanks, who had previously held a top post in the motor industry. When Swindon was designing the standard 204hp diesel shunter, he asked that the fuel tank be placed on top of the engine bonnet in order to give the appearance of a steam locomotive firebox; this displayed his attitude towards diesels. The extra height he sought is evident in a side profile view of Class 03.

Another handicap was Commission insistence on front-end gangway doors for footplate crews when locomotives were operating in multiple. A further dictat was a nose-end for the Type 4s because of the perceived (but erroneous) risk of 'sleeper flicker' affecting drivers during high-speed running where the locomotive had a flat front.

Derby Works wasn't alone when it came to outward appearance. All the railway works were particularly bad at this stage when it came to styling, examples being various classes of EMU and the Hastings line DEMUs. A standard Mark 1 carriage had been produced in 1951 but its interior quickly began to look dated, for example by the continued use of exposed light bulbs. Contractors building DMUs showed more enterprise in both external and internal appearance and fitment.

As with railway-designed locomotives (diesel and SR electric of the 1950s), the Commission's workshops were behind the curve on carriage design too. Fortunately, the Blue Pullman sets to be described in the next chapter, were the inspired results of Metro-Cammell staff, who produced a vehicle interior that taught BR a few lessons when the latter's first Mark 2 carriage appeared in 1964.

In June 1955 BTC Member T. H. Summerson wanted new locomotives to have a 'stimulating' appearance and colleagues lower down the pecking order agreed that design needed a sharper focus as an element of the Modernisation Plan. In August 1956 the BTC set up the Design Panel, a top-level body that was supported by the Design Research Unit (DRU), which handled day-to-day matters.

A small number of external consultants, such as Misha Black and Ted Wilkes, were kept busy, each being allocated a particular class where they acted as the liaison point between the DRU and the contractor. Black was a leading figure in the external appearance of Class 52, whilst Wilkes was responsible for Class 35 'Hymeks' concurrently with the Brush prototype *Falcon* and the BRCW prototype *Lion* before tackling Class 47 and so explaining the family resemblance.

W. Sykes, the SR CM&EE, had decided views on many aspects of Class 33, which was an early post-Pilot Scheme order awarded to BRCW. Whereas the Design Panel 'standard' was vinyl for seat covering, the SR wanted its traditional moquette. This relatively minor detail occupied quite a three-way correspondence between the DRU, Wilkes (the consultant) and Sykes.

By 1961, when orders for the new standard Types 1 and 4 came to be placed, the impact of careful attention to styling was clearly evident. Although the Type 1s soon proved to be a disappointment, due to no prototyping before squadron ordering, the locomotive looked very good!

All parts of the Commission benefited from what can fairly be dubbed the design revolution. New station buildings had a more light and airy environment, with less clutter and better signage and train information displays. Staff uniforms were given a facelift, with station masters no longer sporting homburgs or even top hats at principal stations.

Liveries and embellishments

In April 1956 the BTC approved the adoption of standard Locomotive Green for all types of diesel and electric locomotives with lining out, in the case of main line passenger and mixed-traffic units. It also approved the use of names for locomotives hauling the express passenger trains on the principal routes but left the choice of names to each Area Board, subject to Commission agreement.

The decision to adopt Locomotive Green was the bane of the DRU, who really disliked it. Pilot Scheme classes appeared with horizontal bands in light grey at varying heights and thicknesses to relieve the basic livery, which can be appreciated at its worst in the Hastings DEMUs and early BR-built EMUs.

When advising on the production series 'Deltics', Ted Wilkes proposed a two-tone green scheme. Some experimentation was needed before lime green was chosen for the lower bodyside and this was also applied to Class 35. Wilkes' involvement with Class 47, the new standard Type 4, in 1961 was probably also why the two-tone green idea was taken to its final form, with Sherwood Green as the lower shade.

DRU influence with the Class 52 'Westerns' saw several liveries tried. The class doyen appeared in Desert Sand, a shade rejected for the AC electrics of Classes 81 to 85. Turquoise was considered but rejected. Locomotives emerged from Swindon in Locomotive Green, much to the chagrin on the DRU, who hated the colour, but coaching stock red was also applied. The latter found favour with the WR's Regional Manager, Stanley Raymond, and he unilaterally ordered all further examples to appear thus. It was over a year before the BR CM&EE found out! One example, No D1015, had a unique livery of Golden Ochre, produced by mixing BR Pipework Orange with GWR Chocolate Brown.

The manner in which the livery for the AC electrics was reached has an interesting aspect. Several colours were considered but Caledonian Railway Blue (actually Prussian Blue) was decided upon. The problem was that pictorial evidence showed inconsistency in the shade. The artist and historian Cuthbert Hamilton-Ellis was consulted because he had been brought up close to the Caledonian and solved the riddle by saying the shade of Prussian Blue varied according to how much white lead (a constituent of paint) St Rollox Works put into each batch of paint it made. On the strength of this, the DRU came up with its own shade, which it referred to as Electric Blue. This was also used for the Glasgow suburban EMUs and was not applied to DC electric locomotives.

When it came to naming, the Western was the only Region to go to town on this, with all its diesel-hydraulic and a handful of diesel-electric Type 4s so adorned. The Regions operating the East Coast line decided to name the production 'Deltics', Class 55, with the NER and ScR opting for army regiments, whilst the ER chose famous racehorses in a throwback to the names carried by LNER Class A3 Pacifics. The LMR chose to name a few of its EE Type 4s after merchant ships that were frequent visitors to the Port of Liverpool. Naming then dropped out of favour for two decades.

Then in 1964 BR launched its 'XP64' trainset, where the locomotive body was painted Rail Blue, which was then also applied to multiple units and coaching stock. As the majority of the traction and rolling stock fleet had been dealt with by 1970, the end of the period envisaged for the Modernisation Plan, some felt that the uniformity was boring.

Chapter 9

Inter-city DMUs

Chapter 6 identified four separate markets for DMUs, which might be defined as a self-propelled trainset. In that chapter, designs for suburban, branch and cross-country duties were considered but discussion of the types built for inter-city work have been reserved for this chapter.

First, Technical Committee Members had been keeping abreast with developments in express trains on the Continent, assisted by Dr den Hollander, the head of Netherlands Railways, who was a key representative on railway modernisation. One such was the Spanish Talgo trainset, which was under development in 1954, and the Committee decided to monitor progress.

Talgos have a very low profile, being mounted on small running gear, to enable them to take corners at a faster rate than conventional stock. They followed general Continental practice by having a power car as part of the trainset, rather than a separate locomotive or with underfloor powertrains. In June 1956 an update reported that Metro-Cammell was considering acquiring a licence to build Talgos in Britain but the Committee noted that none had yet entered commercial service in Spain.

Blue Pullman, White Elephant
In June 1954 the BTC acquired total control of the Pullman Car Co. Despite this, the Commission decided to leave it as a self-contained, semi-autonomous entity but it was viewed with suspicion by the railway unions even though Pullman employees were union members.

At its meeting on 20 January 1955 the Commission debated how to get the best out of its acquisition. Before outlining the discussion at that meeting, the views of our old friend and part-time BTC Member, H. P. Barker, as set out in a memo to the Commission dated 11 October 1954 on possibilities for exploiting the brand are quoted here.

> I think there is a need to establish as quickly as possible and
> perhaps in advance of the main re-equipment programme, a new

type of 'prestige' inter-city service, characterised by the highest passenger comfort and reasonable though not excessive speed.

1 – British Railways need to do something that will catch the imagination of the public and give a visible demonstration of the new potentialities of rail travel.

2 – It may be commercially desirable to show our air competitors that they stand little chance of attracting inter-city passengers from us, at least below 200 miles. The attitude of the public towards internal air travel remains in the formative stage and could be warped away from it as in France.

Two instruments have been placed in our hands recently and these are:

The possibility of using the Pullman name which I believe has great sales value, the arrival of the multiple-unit diesel train and consequent upon above, the possibility of reversing trains, maintaining a shuttle-like service and thereby achieving an intensive use of the equipment.

I suggest that the Commission staff and the Regional Managers should examine the possibility of introducing a series of named Pullman trains, eg the 'Birmingham Belle,' the 'Manchester Belle', the 'Leeds Belle', operating once or twice per day in each direction. The trains would be two-class probably with a supplementary charge and to modern Pullman standards.

Mechanically, I suggest that the trains should be of the multiple-unit diesel-type, with maximum running speeds of say 85mph and sufficient power reserve to be able to make up reasonable lost time. The train would be reversible and I envisage would be serviced after each round trip; that is to say, if such a train ran on the Midland route to Birmingham, it would depart from the same Euston platform at which it arrived, and perhaps not more than half an hour afterwards. This would mean I suppose some new organisation for servicing the train on arrival but this cannot be a mighty problem; if the airlines can do it, so can we!

From the staffing point of view, I picture that the train would be run by the Pullman Co staffs.

We are preparing at Swindon to build the inter-city trains for Glasgow to Edinburgh and Birmingham to Swansea. I do not know if the mechanical design of these trains (ie the chassis) would be suitable for the purpose envisaged but it might be that the design and construction of these trains could be a joint enterprise between Swindon and the Pullman Car Co.

I know that there is some prejudice in railway circles against the Pullman Co as such. If the Commission seriously intends to develop the Pullman principle, this may be the way to go.

Of course the DMUs to which Barker referred as under construction at Swindon were unsuitable for several reasons, not least because their maximum speed was only 70mph. Nevertheless, his memo provided a springboard for thoughts within headquarters and the Regions, which proved to be completely polarised.

The ER view was that it couldn't recommend any additional Pullman services, though the possibility would be kept in mind. It certainly did, because it introduced a 'Sheffield Pullman' from King's Cross in autumn 1958 when Regional boundary changes effectively transferred the Marylebone to Sheffield route to the LMR from the start of the year. The Region noted that it would soon be necessary to replace the existing hauled Pullman coaches and the possibility of a DMU format should be considered.

No more favourable response came from the LMR, which saw operating problems on the Euston to Birmingham route. In fact the Region had no plans at all for Pullman services and wished to see the performance of the inter-city DMUs being designed at Swindon before committing itself.

Whilst the NER thought there might be a case for Pullman services between Hull, Leeds and Liverpool, it doubted their viability. This was because of the lower seating capacity and the deterrent affect of supplementary fares, and the Region concluded that the best prospect was for services into, and out of, London.

The ScR gave Barker's idea a 'thumbs down' because it judged the services from Glasgow to Edinburgh and from these cities to Aberdeen to be unsuitable. It also ruled out use between Glasgow, Edinburgh and England, seemingly having overlooked the existing 'Queen of Scots' Pullman that linked Leeds with Edinburgh and Glasgow!

The SR drew attention to its existing use of Pullman trains, which it did not propose to expand. No cross-country services existed on which Pullmans might be introduced.

Surprisingly, the WR expressed no comment at all on the introduction of Pullman services. It merely provided chapter and verse as to the unsuitability of the new inter-city DMUs being designed at Swindon for adaptation to Pullman sets.

Just why the Regions were so disinterested is unclear because the Chief of Operating Services on the British Railways Central Staff was quite positive. He saw Pullman trains as a further weapon in the fight against the private car and suggested the Regions be asked to prepare schemes for the trains, which would have to be additional to those already running because of the issue of lower seating capacity; London to Manchester was the main route identified.

So far as the Chief of Commercial Services was concerned, the running of high-speed trains with special accommodation would have commercial advantages, provided it was not to the detriment of ordinary services. He was concerned that running additional services might not generate sufficient additional revenue to cover the new total costs. Like his headquarters' colleague, he suggested the Regions should work up one or two proposals.

Returning to the January 1955 Commission meeting, the Members thought that the first objective of any change would be to use these services to develop the railway passenger traffics which could be carried at a profit.

It appeared that any development policy would have to follow two stages. The first, short term, one would consist of testing the possibilities of traffic development by running additional services, particularly over routes not associated with Pullman services. The second stage, a longer term one, would largely be governed by the results of the experiment and might involve substantial new construction of Pullman stock.

Stage 1 would depend on conducting an experiment with existing Pullman stock over a new route or routes. The SR, ER and NER regions had a number of regular Pullman services, whilst the 'Queen of Scots' ran into the Scottish region. With no such service on the LMR or WR, it was therefore the possibility of experimenting on these regions that attention was first directed.

The running of additional Pullman services, however successful in attracting new traffic, was almost certain to have an effect on the patronage of railway restaurant cars. This would impact on the interests of the Commission's Hotel & Catering services in two ways. First, it would reduce their gross takings, perhaps necessitating a curtailment of the service which they provided. Secondly, it raised difficult staff questions.

Railway restaurant car staff tended to regard the extension of Pullman services with some antagonism. This was particularly marked after nationalisation when the Pullman Car Co was still in private hands. It was still likely to be a significant factor, partly because Pullman Car Co rates and conditions of service were rather less favourable to the staff than those of railway restaurant car staff, and partly because there was a fear that the extension of Pullman services would affect some of the most remunerative of railway catering services, leading to loss of earnings by senior staff and some risk of redundancy.

With these general considerations as a background, there were two possible ways of making the experiment. The first was to run the cars on established services for an experimental period. In this connection, the Regional Managers suggested that one first and one third class car be run on each of the following routes:

Wolverhampton to Paddington
Cheltenham to Paddington
Manchester to Euston via Wilmslow and Crewe, returning from Euston to
    Manchester via Stoke
Manchester to Euston via Stoke, and back to Manchester via Crewe and
    Wilmslow.

Passengers in the cars would retain their seats throughout the journey; British Railways restaurant car facilities would, for the period of the experiment, remain on substantially the same scale as at present, and the Pullman staff would not canvass the train for custom of passengers wishing to be served with meals or drinks.

An experiment conducted on these lines was seen to have three main advantages. First, it could be made without incurring additional passenger train mileage. Secondly, it would enable the Pullman Car Co to 'feel its way' over new routes and gradually to build up staff based on the provincial centres served. Finally, it could be introduced without delay.

The principal disadvantage was that it would be necessary to make some curtailment of the existing restaurant car facilities available on the trains, and would lead to an intensification of the staff objection to the introduction of the new services.

The second possible method was to run an all-Pullman train. Unfortunately the only coaching stock that could be made available for this experiment without disruption of established services was limited to the cars employed on the 'Devon Belle'.

This meant that only one such train could be run, and the most suitable service to try would be one leaving Swansea at 7.45am for Paddington, calling at Port Talbot, Cardiff and Newport and returning later from Paddington. Existing trains over routes suitable for the experiment were already well loaded general-purpose services, and a Pullman train with its limited accommodation would be no substitute for them.

The advantages of this alternative were that it would not affect the composition of the existing services in the early stages of the experiment, would not therefore have any marked effect on railway catering services, and finally the impact on the public of the running of a new full Pullman service was likely to be far greater than that of occasional cars.

The disadvantages were that it involved additional train mileage, it would test only one route, it would take the Pullman Car Co some time to make the necessary staff and rolling stock arrangements for the running of a full train, and it would not be possible to start the new service much before Easter 1955.

It was the intention that Pullman supplements would accord with those already in force on other routes. In view of the staff aspect referred to above, consultation with the National Union of Railwaymen (NUR) had started.

The Commission judged that, as a commercial venture, there was little to choose between the two alternatives, but the operation of a new Pullman train was likely to have the least disturbing effects on the business and staff of the BTC catering services, and so this alternative was preferred. Delayed due to a footplatemen's strike, the experimental 'South Wales Pullman' was inaugurated on 27 June 1955, formed from eight chocolate & cream coaches and worked by a Swansea Landore 'Castle' class steam locomotive in each direction.

Beyond the experiment described above, the Commission turned its attention to the second stage as foreshadowed in Barker's memo, where it was suggested that there should be a series of named Pullman trains between cities.

Two separate ideas emerged. The first derived from Barker's suggestion, and was for high-speed DMUs between cities, which would be additional to existing services, expressly designed to meet competition from other forms of transport. The second possibility came as a volte face by the Regional Managers of the Eastern and North Eastern, and was to replace existing steam-hauled Pullman trains by diesel Pullman vehicles.

The Commission reviewed these two approaches. If the first were developed, it would be desirable for one or more Regions, in consultation with the Pullman Car Co and the Commission's hotel and catering services, to prepare 'pilot' schemes for consideration, but it was judged prudent to defer the preparation of such pilot schemes until the results of the experiment with the new 'South Wales Pullman' were available.

Alternatively, progressing the ER/NER proposal would require the Pullman Car Co and the Regions concerned to prepare a joint report. This could proceed immediately, as it related to existing Pullman services and would not be substantially affected by the outcome of the 'South Wales Pullman'.

The meeting resolved to go forward with both these options, as well as the experimental 'South Wales Pullman' referred to above.

In typical BTC style, a committee was set up, the Diesel Multiple-unit Mainline Express Services Committee, under the chairmanship of H. H. Phillips, the Assistant Regional Manager of the WR, who had chaired the Forms of Motive Power Sub-Committee in 1954. Against a remit of a self-powered trainset, the Committee gave consideration to a wide range of aspects of the subject, including air conditioning and no standing passengers to be allowed, and reported in July 1956. Committee members had travelled widely across Europe to study practice on other railways.

There was a very detailed consideration of the provision of tractive power, starting with whether motors should be underfloor, frame mounted or bogie mounted and whether each vehicle should be powered or power concentrated in a few vehicles. Thus a seven-car formation might have 14 engines of 150bhp to provide 2,100 in total or 10 each of 200bhp. Frame mounting was ruled out because the only example of such practice was in Italy, where vehicles were 80ft long; British vehicles would be 63ft 6in. Vehicle weights for various configurations were carefully calculated.

Any form of power under a passenger-carrying vehicle was judged to be liable to generate vibration and intrusive noise and the preference was for 1,000hp at each end of the trainset. For the LMR, each set was recommended to be powered by a MAN diesel of 1,000bhp at each end, linked to GEC electrical equipment. By contrast, the WR sets were to have hydraulic transmission, using either a MAN/Voith or Maybach/Mekydro powertrain. Auxiliary diesels of 354bhp would provide power for the train equipment.

These power configurations were calculated to result in a total weight of 49 tons for the diesel-electric variant and 28½ tons for the diesel-hydraulic at respective costs of £71,000 and £61,300, a clear advantage in favour of the latter type. Perhaps understandably, the Committee made a strong recommendation for the diesel-hydraulic variant, not least because some Trans Europ Express sets on the Continent were so powered. Additionally, the saving of 20 tons would assist the WR eight-car sets in attaining better timings, which would not be an issue on the LMR's six-car formations.

A report forming part of the chairman's conference on the Modernisation Plan in September 1956 referred to the proposed diesel Pullman sets.

LMR deployment of its first-class-only variant was to be between Manchester Central and St Pancras, whilst the WR was to diagram its two-class sets from

Birmingham Snow Hill and Bristol Temple Meads to Paddington. The ER was invited to draw up a proposal for its Marylebone to Sheffield Victoria route.

One aspect of the project that was revised was its title. At its most wordy, it became 'Diesel Multiple-Unit Main-Line De Luxe Express' in BTC papers! Eventually the title of 'Blue Pullman' was adopted, which was based on the paint scheme of Nanking Blue. The Works Committee gave its recommendation to the Commission in November 1956 and on the 29th approval was given to the awarding of a contract to Metro-Cammell for 36 vehicles to form five trainsets, two for the LMR and three for the WR in the sum of £1.215 million.

Vehicle width was an issue because the WR loading gauge was more generous than the LMR's but the Commission insisted on a standard width for these five experimental units. An added complication was the cramped layout at Manchester Central and this dictated adoption of the 'C1' loading gauge. The experimental nature of the project also caused the BTC to conclude that hydraulic transmission should not be used. Staff union consultation was to be carried out quickly at headquarters.

Pullman developments were not confined to the 'Blue Pullmans' because in September 1957 the Commission sanctioned the replacement of 44 locomotive-hauled carriages by a like number of new ones, which were to be of the most modern design. During the same month, the Commission accepted that a realistic date for commencement of the new services on the LMR would be spring 1959 or, if more convenient, an introduction in the summer 1959 timetable.

At the start of 1958 BRCW offered an alternative trainset. It is possible that news of the order to Metro-Cammell had leaked across Birmingham and BRCW proposed using a 2,150hp Sulzer engine. The BTC decided to await the outcome of the trials with the sets already on order before giving this new proposal any further consideration.

Design work progressed very slowly and a flavour of the fact that the project was in trouble emerges from the BTC minutes of July 1959 because the Works Committee had only just finalised details of the vehicles. Costs had escalated and the Commission now called for a reassessment of the financial results of the programme, both regarding the Regions and the Pullman Car Co, after financial arrangements with the latter had been finalised.

The subject was discussed again at Commission level in March 1960 and it was noted that trial running was under way and timetabled operation planned to start on the LMR in June. Even at this late stage, these arrangements were subject to an agreement with the NUR on the staffing of trains, notably catering personnel. Over three years had elapsed since the project had been sanctioned but the staffing issue remained unresolved.

The 'Midland Pullman' began running on 4 July and achieved both very high standards of punctuality and much favourable comment from the travelling public. The trains were air-conditioned throughout, a feature that would not be provided in standard coaching stock until 1971, with first-class passengers having reclining seats and a full at-seat service. WR 'Blue Pullman' sets running between Wolverhampton/Birmingham and Bristol and Paddington were put into service on 12 September. On the Midland Line, timings were sharp. The morning up service took just under 3¼ hours and was even quicker heading north in the evening. Passing Bedford, the 49.6 miles up to town were timed for 84mph, which included an uphill section at 1 in 200. The WR was less adventurous. For example, with one stop the down 'Bristol Pullman' was 15 minutes slower than the best non-stop steam.

Sadly, the trainsets rode very poorly, despite the Swiss design of bogie performing admirably on the Continent. This was the second instance of a good-riding Continental bogie design proving unsuitable on British Railways track and spoke much about the state of permanent way here. Urgent work was put in hand on bogie suspension to resolve the issue and improvements were made.

By the end of 1961 the WR had arranged Pullman workings so that all three sets had daily diagrams. Not so on the LMR, where there was only one daily diagram, giving an uneconomic 50% utilisation. Even deploying the one set in use on a mid-day fill-in turn to Nottingham was eventually abandoned due to trade union restrictions. Completion of electrification to Euston brought the sensible move to transfer the whole fleet to the WR but the experiment was never extended, though the LMR did get 29 hauled Pullman carriages for new services along the electrified West Coast line to Liverpool Lime Street as well as Manchester Piccadilly.

Trans-Pennine inter-city DMUs
Consideration of the traction requirements for conversion of the Hull to Liverpool trans-Pennine inter-city services to diesel was discussed at a meeting of the Technical Committee on 29 April 1955. Whereas the newly-electrified Woodhead route was primarily used to convey coal westwards, the more northerly Leeds, Huddersfield and Manchester corridor was the main artery for passenger traffic. It, too, was steeply graded, one example being the climb west from Huddersfield where trains faced eight miles uphill at mainly 1 in 105. There was, however, no agreement on how to deploy diesel power.

One faction proposed the building of a two-car prototype, using a Paxman 6ZHX engine of 450bhp under each vehicle, married to a main generator that would then power two traction motors on one bogie. Derby Works cobbled together such a unit from two 1920s carriages, suitably converted and with driving cabs at one end of each coach. This emerged in 1956 and ran extensive trials but failed to win wider support and never ran in service. Using the available power at rail, rather than the installed figure, the power-to-weight ratio worked out at a respectable 7.2hp per ton.

The Technical Committee felt, however, that using the new standard-pattern powertrain, incorporating two 150bhp BUT engines, would give roughly the same power-to-weight ratio, after allowing for the inherently higher transmission efficiency of mechanical over electrical drivetrains and consequential lower vehicle weights. As the sponsoring Region for the proposed revamped service, the NER was unhappy and wanted more power; it also wanted to await the availability of a new Albion engine of 230bhp.

It was not until April 1959 that the Commission sanctioned provisionally the building of 51 inter-city vehicles as part of the 1960 building programme, comprising 34 motor coaches, nine trailers and eight trailer-buffets to provide a pool for seven serviceable trainsets for the trans-Pennine route. That authority was only provisional because Members were unhappy at the excessive number of spare vehicles for maintenance being sought and wanted this brought down from 17.6% to 15%. The North Eastern Area Board was told to resubmit the proposal if the Region could not live with this level of maintenance spares.

Design and construction was the responsibility of Swindon, with input from the BR Design Panel. The latter produced a handsome front end, clearly based on the Glasgow suburban 'Blue Train' EMUs, with wrap-around windscreens. The sets were formed with a driving motor coach at each end and two non-driving motor coaches, plus a trailer and a trailer buffet. Installed power was 1,840hp and the power-to-weight ratio at the rail was about 7.5hp per ton or 8.2 gross. A most unusual feature was the preparation of limited hot food in what was dubbed the griddle car, rather than it being just a buffet.

The new sets began to emerge from Swindon during the second half of 1960, allocated to Hull, and the trans-Pennine timetable was recast from January 1961 with, basically, an hourly service between Leeds City and Manchester Exchange, with most trains running through to Liverpool Lime Street. Whilst most were formed of the new inter-city DMUs, four each way daily ran between Newcastle and Liverpool and were formed of EE Type 4 diesels and hauled stock. Timings were cut by 20 minutes and it was claimed that patronage over the route doubled by the end of the year.

Birmingham to South Wales upgrade

With construction of the trans-Pennine DMUs ending, in spring 1960 the WR cast around for another project to keep Swindon Works occupied. The Region decided that the inter-city DMUs that had been operating its Birmingham Snow Hill to South Wales route for barely two years were 'unsatisfactory'. These 18 vehicles had only entered service late in 1957 and utilisation was generally poor because too many vehicles had been procured. Interestingly, the ScR, which was operating identical DMUs between Edinburgh and Glasgow, and near-identical ones from Glasgow to Ayr, made no similar complaint!

The WR now wanted 40 vehicles for 10 sets, comprising 20 power cars, 15 trailers and five trailer-buffets, which would be formed into either three- or four-car sets. It was envisaged that train mileage would be unaltered but power car mileage would be reduced, offering an annual saving of £12,000. A return of 30% on the additional outlay was predicted by virtue of replacing the existing DMUs and steam rolling stock, which seems too good to be true in retrospect! The calculation of a paltry 2% on the total investment was dismissed 'because most of the vehicles being displaced were suitable for use elsewhere'.

Although the BTC had given outline approval in May 1960 for design work to begin, it asked that a much clearer overall financial statement should be submitted as quickly as possible; this was in view of the necessity to submit proposals to the Minister of Transport under the newly-implemented arrangements for significant capital expenditure. On the question of the design, BTC Member Summerson suggested it should be looked at from the point of view of these vehicles still being up to date in 20 years time. It was November when the Chief Accountant came up with the figure of a 55% return on net investment and approval was given.

During its consideration of the scheme, the Works Committee noted that the WR's existing 18 vehicles had been sent on loan to the ScR, which felt it would be difficult to deploy them permanently because of their non-standard control equipment precluding operation in multiple with other than their Scottish equivalents. The WR said it would consider redeploying the cast-offs on forthcoming Chester and Central Wales schemes but neither of these new proposals could be submitted until the request for the new inter-city sets had been agreed. Surprisingly, the Works Committee decided that the WR's proposal should be treated as a special case and dealt with as a matter of urgency.

For the record, the original 18 vehicles stayed in Scotland. The loan became a permanent transfer in November 1961, with four three-car sets for deployment between Edinburgh Princes Street and Glasgow Central (the existing Scottish allocation worked between Waverley and Queen Street) and two three-car sets augmenting the Glasgow St Enoch to Ayr and Girvan pool of similar vehicles.

It is also worth pointing out how Commission attitudes had evolved during the first five years of dieselisation. When the Birmingham to South Wales proposal was put forward in 1954, the WR wanted 18 vehicles to form six sets. Of these, only four were envisaged as being used in daily service, operating two return trips in six-car formations. Thus 50% of the stock was maintenance spares. By the time of the WR's Birmingham Area DMU submission in January 1957, 21% of the vehicles sought were spares. Two years later, the NER was told to cut its requirement for the trans-Pennine modernisation to a maximum of 15% spare vehicles. Money for modernisation was not limitless and the capital outlay on schemes had to be spent with due economy, not profligacy.

These were the last of the First Generation DMUs to be built and, indeed, brought carriage construction at Swindon to an end. They benefited from the use of the new B4 trailer and B5 motor bogie, which gave a superior ride compared to previous DMUs. The sets were gangwayed throughout, using the Pullman gangway, and had a much better style of front end than the sets they were to replace. Thus two four-car sets could be coupled and passengers given access to the buffet located in only one set.

The same powertrain as installed in the trans-Pennine DMUs was fitted, that is the Albion 230bhp diesel and four-speed gearbox. Each driving vehicle was powered, whilst the centre cars were trailers; the installed power was 920bhp for a trainset of roughly 145 tons but maximum speed was only 70mph. Whereas this was not a problem for the trans-Pennine route, where 75mph was the line speed west of Leeds until the 1980s, 70mph was hardly likely to be a suitable upper limit for attaining the BTC aim of inter-city trains *averaging* at least that rate!

It was not only in the sphere of road performance that these new DMUs were inadequate for inter-city work. The first set emerged in February 1963 and, by the time the order had been completed, services between Birmingham and South Wales had migrated from the former GWR route from Snow Hill to Cheltenham in favour of the ex LMSR line south from New Street. As a result, the newcomers worked as far as Derby but Regional boundary changes quickly saw the WR redeploy them elsewhere.

All the references during the procurement phase in 1960 refer purely to use between Birmingham and South Wales, no doubt the 10 four-car sets being called for to displace not only the 1957 series DMUs but also steam-hauled diagrams. Redeployment came in the shape of turns from Cardiff to Bristol and onwards to Portsmouth. This was much more 'cross-country' than inter-city and the DMUs' performance characteristics suited the route quite well. Eventually the sets moved to Reading depot for Paddington outer-suburban work and here, again, 70mph was not really adequate for journeys as far as Oxford along the fast lines.

The class did not only bring down the curtain on Swindon carriage works. It seems highly likely that the WR only pushed for the new DMUs in order to keep production there going for a little longer. The BTC should have taken the opportunity in 1960 to review passenger flows between Birmingham and South Wales and downgrade the ex GWR route then, concentrating traffic on the former Midland line, which it did three years later.

Paddington had bamboozled the Commission into letting it build replica 'V200' locomotives on a promise of estimated costs that proved to be 40% adrift. With steam locomotive production at Swindon ending in 1956, the Region had a sudden, unforeseen and urgent need to replace a number of heavy freight locomotives, for which no diesel was suitable. The answer was for Swindon, no longer building heavy freight steam traction by then, to restart production, rather than workshops that were still turning out the type adding on another batch. Such were the vagaries in Commission decision-making, and the following chapter will consider the implications.

Chapter 10

Diesel deliveries

Mechanisms for modernising
As has been seen already, the Commission's response to any situation was to form a committee. To be fair, it was sensible to have a modernisation co-ordinating group for the plans of the six Regions, which would act in a way not possible for the Works Committee, whose function was largely project-focused ahead of procurement whilst the Technical Committee was more one of keeping an eye on engineering developments. Thus the Modernisation Plan Steering Committee came into being in 1955 and was chaired by the Secretary-General of the Commission's General Staff, by now Major-General Llewellyn Wansbrough-Jones, who had recently succeeded General Sir Daril Watson.

In July 1956 the engineering staff prepared a report titled 'Selection of Diesel Types' for the Technical Committee, which went to the Modernisation Steering Group to guide the Regions on the characteristics of diesel performance, which differed from steam. The objective was to provide guidance on the selection of types of locomotive as part of the compilation of area schemes for dieselisation. An unanswered question was whether two Type 2s in multiple offered greater flexibility than a single Type 4. Another possibility raised was to have Types 2 and 3 geared differently for passenger or freight duties.

The report also revised diesel power categories from the original three to five with the addition of a mid power range of 1,500 to 1,750hp and a high power range of 3,000 to 3,600hp. No preference was expressed as to electric or hydraulic transmission or two-stroke versus four-stroke cycle engines and the engineers looked forward to technical development of the diesel engine.

The engineers' report formed part of a document on traffic policy which went to the Area Boards and they then submitted proposals from October. Each Region wanted to be sure of getting at least its fair share of the modernisation pot and each drew up motive power requirements which were assembled into a massive document in April 1957 setting out passenger trains for the future.

The proposals called for 5,333 route-miles of electrification, acquiring 2,333 diesel main line locomotives by 1962 and 5,126 DMU vehicles. Of course such a combined programme was beyond the capacity of British Railways and private contractors combined to deliver, but this was mere detail!

Before delving into the proposals, the thorny issue of train manning was put in hand in June 1956. It was to be November 1957 before a draft agreement covering diesel and electric locomotives and DMUs was agreed and this came into force in January 1958.

A further issue, which cannot be understated, was the technical competence of the mechanical engineering staff. Their colleagues on the electrical side were already up to speed with matters arising from modernisation, save for the switch from 1,500V DC to 25kV AC line supply. A fascinating insight into the degree of understanding is provided by a question put by E. S. Cox, the head of locomotive and rolling stock design on the British Railways Central Staff, to a meeting of the Institution of Electrical Engineers in July 1958.

Commenting on the relatively high speed of the continuous traction motor rating of the prototype *Deltic* compared to EE's 2,000hp design, Cox asked whether he was correct in thinking that the higher the continuous tractive effort then the freer from trouble and maintenance were the traction motors likely to be.

By then Cox ought to have known that a motor's continuous rating was a product of its design and, as regards the locomotive, the motor/bogie gear ratio. As dieselisation progressed, the same EE traction motor, with the same gearing, would be fitted to three classes, one of 1,750hp, one of 2,700hp and the production 'Deltics' of 3,300hp.

As an aside, when it came to locomotive design and construction, if the unit was an electric the Chief Electrical Engineer led, with his mechanical opposite number assisting with the mechanical parts, such as bodywork and bogies. For diesels, the electrical side acted as support to the CME.

At Regional motive power depots and in the workshops, staff at all levels had to be migrated from steam traction maintenance to the regimes needed for a diesel. During 1958 there had been arguments concerning the poor availability of the six large prototype diesels of pre-nationalisation design and naturally the LMR rebutted allegations that this was due to incompetence by local shed staff. All Regions endeavoured to have appropriate facilities – equipment and manpower – ready for the squadron arrival of the new traction generally.

The end of the Pilot Scheme
A short digression is needed now to set the scene for what was to follow.

In his various writings, Cox has shown antipathy to the GWR and the attempts after nationalisation to retain a degree of detached autonomy from the RE and BTC. Keith Grand, its Regional Manager until elevation to become a

Commission Member in 1959, and Reginald Hanks, the chairman of the Western Area Board, had lobbied hard for Swindon to build its own prototype main line diesel-hydraulics. The Region grasped the ScR's coat tails for the first inter-city DMUs to be built, Swindon carrying out the design and construction. Grand also got permission to paint rakes of carriages for the Region's named trains into GWR chocolate and cream livery.

With steam locomotive construction winding down on British Railways, in spring 1956 the WR suddenly discovered it urgently needed 30 new '9F' heavy freight engines to replace life-expired Class 28XXs. No diesel was judged suitable. On 10 April the Technical Committee considered the situation and was prepared to let the request go ahead because no diesels had yet been delivered, let alone assessed.

The matter went to the Commission for approval but Chairman Robertson was distinctly unhappy and bounced it back to the Works Committee. Eventually Robertson was persuaded on the basis that no current diesel design would do. Of course the order went to Swindon, which kept the metal bashers busy until diesel-hydraulic construction got into full swing!

During the planning stages of modernisation, in January 1955 the Technical Committee had proposed that it would be sensible to try out a range of diesel locomotive designs and then to standardise on the most successful after three years. The ones chosen for this study were based on logical parameters and to allow the railways' workshops to build up experience. By April 1956 the Technical Committee changed its mind and felt it was not necessary to wait for three years before placing further orders.

At its meeting in July 1956 discussing traffic policy referred to above, the Commission's resolve to see the three-year trial through was also weakening. Members discussed the purchase of additional main line diesel locomotives and expressed a willingness to consider requests for a number of these without further trials, provided that there was sufficient technical evidence to show that the type of locomotive fully and without doubt was able to meet relevant requirements. These requirements included an economic justification for the replacement of steam.

Cox has blamed others than the engineers for this volte face but the first hole in the dyke came from the Technical Committee, which was composed of engineers! Cox's superior, R. C. Bond, the CME on the Central Staff, produced a report in 1957 entitled 'Limitation of Variety', which sought a narrower range of designs for future orders. This attempt to limit unproven equipment came to nought. It was to be 1960 before contractors were invited to propose designs for a new standard Type 1 and a 2,750hp Type 4. Both were ordered in quantity straight off the drawing board and both suffered serious engine problems, among other issues.

Deliveries of Pilot Scheme designs began in June 1957 and were not completed until the end of 1959. Even before the first example had turned a wheel in traffic, the highly-laudable idea of trial running ahead of standardisation on a few designs had been abandoned.

Illustrating the avalanche of orders, on 19 September 1957 the BTC reviewed the state of play regarding main line diesel procurement, particularly in the context of the 1959 building programme. By now Regional schemes had a requirement for 782 locomotives for that year's programme and it was agreed that this exceeded the capacity of its own and contractors' shops to deliver. Even so, outline approval was given to ordering between 750 to 800 machines for 1959, subject to the usual Works Committee submissions to the Commission for approval.

Such was the desperation to press forward with the elimination of steam that it was agreed to possibly make use of some companies not at present associated with locomotive building. If ever that was a recipe for disaster! The meeting also charged the General Staff with balancing Regional demands to ensure equality of treatment.

Diesel-hydraulics

The WR was quick off the mark in seeking authority to proceed with its plans for the elimination of steam west of Newton Abbot, termed Area 1. After a 'softening-up' process during 1956, the Region's proposals had been discussed by the Works Committee prior to coming before the Commission on 28 February 1957 when 52 Type 2 and 64 (later 63) Type 4 diesel-hydraulics were sought to replace 246 steam locomotives; of the 64, 30 were to be built by Swindon and 34 by NBL. The tenor of the BTC minute suggests a reluctance to proceed with more orders for this form of traction because of the lack of UK experience but the promising results in Germany were noted.

Back in 1954 the use of diesel-hydraulic drivetrains was clearly stated to be an experiment but here the WR wanted to go into squadron production. One of the aims of modernisation was for diesels to operate across Regional boundaries in a way not done with steam. Footplate crew had to be trained on each type of motive power on which they were expected to work and Regions other than the Western were not happy at having the expense of this training imposed by the WR's choice of non-standard traction. It has been claimed that this was part of the policy of keeping that Region functioning in semi-independence from the rest of British Railways.

In addition, the Commission accepted the great importance attached by the Western Area board to this proposal and its confidence in it. Essential detailed records of cost of operation and maintenance of the new locomotives had to be kept in a manner that would give true comparison with similar data for other alternative types.

Demonstrating Commission reluctance on this proposal, Chairman Robertson wrote to his opposite number on Germany's railways for feedback about diesel-hydraulic performance there. Despite this coming back favourably, when he referred to the preliminary requirements of the WR for 190 diesel locomotives for Area 2 (Bristol), he said the Commission were likely to take the view that these should have electric transmission.

If Robertson had known then just how much the diesel-hydraulic Type 4s were to cost, he would almost certainly not have agreed to them, which was his view when the matter did come up during a Commission meeting in 1959.

In Chapter 5 we saw that the WR's Regional Manager had claimed that Swindon could build a 'V200' (Class 42 under TOPS numbering) for £72,000, whereas the NBL quote for its proposed design of Type 4 (Class 41) was £86,000. It is not possible now to determine how the figure of £72,000 had been derived but by the February 1957 submission for a further 64 examples, Swindon's unit price had risen in under two years to match NBL's £86,000.

Both were certainly well short of the true figure, which was over £100,000. This emerged when NBL quoted £111,000 each for 34 of the 64 Type 4s in the February 1957 submission, and came to a head at the time construction costs for Swindon's subsequent Type 4 design (Class 52) was put under the microscope. Hence not only was the Swindon variant of the 'V200' more expensive than NBL's more traditional design of Class 41 but also of comparable diesel-electric designs and this wiped out one of the arguments for diesel-hydraulic transmission. Concurrently, EE was having its price of £100,000 each for 10 diesel-electrics (Class 40) snapped up for the LMR, NER and ScR.

It now seems astounding that the Works Committee approved the order with NBL for the 34 (later reduced to 33) locomotives to Swindon's design in view of the extra cost over a diesel-electric equivalent, especially as R. C. Bond, who had proposed the diesel-hydraulic trial, was a Committee Member; money no object! A BR contracts officer has observed that the overriding principle was the engineers got what they wanted. Chairman Robertson was very unhappy at the state of affairs.

Swindon's new 2,700hp Type 4 (Class 52) was on the drawing board in 1959 for the WR Area 2 scheme, and this was to be the swansong for large diesel-hydraulics. A memo from the General Staff dated 6 April 1959 dealing with the 1960 locomotive build programme reported a shift in WR policy as follows:

'Since the WR have now recommended the use of diesel-electric in Area No 4 (Birmingham), they consider that this scheme merits consideration in conjunction with the other regions in the allocation of locomotives.'

The same memo also referred to four of the Pilot Scheme types – NBL Types 1 and 4 and the Type 2s from EE and Metrovick – excluded from re-order.

It will be useful to see the ending of Type 4 diesel-hydraulic procurement. In July 1959 the Works Committee reviewed fresh Regional proposals and Table 8 sets out the position for the combined requirements of the WR's West of England and Bristol areas.

Table 8 WR diesel locomotive requirements for combined Areas 1 and 2

	Type 4	Type 4	Type 3	Type 1 and 2	Total
Power (hp)	2,700	2,000-2,200	1,700	800-1,000	
Required	74	76	32	94	*276*
Authorised	–	76	45	58	*179*
Additional required	74	–	Note 1	44 (Note 2)	*118*

Notes

1 – 13 locomotives extra were to be absorbed in the Area 3 South Wales scheme.
2 – The difference between the number required and those authorised was only 36 but eight of the Type 1s already authorised were not required for the composite scheme and were to be absorbed in a further area scheme.

At this meeting the Committee authorised the construction of 931 diesel-electrics for other Regions and 179 diesel-hydraulics for the WR. Of the 179, 129 were for the West of England Area 1, and 50 in advance of Bristol Area 2 and Bristol/Birmingham.

The WR had now decided that the close integration of traffic working between its Areas 1 and 2 meant that it would be sensible to merge these schemes. As a result the total requirements for the composite scheme was put at 276 locomotives as shown in the accompanying table. Note that the Region received Commission approval for 74 of the new design of 2,700hp diesel-hydraulics.

Next the Area Board produced a memo to the Works Committee dated 31 August 1960 for Area 3 which covered South Wales and lines to Paddington and Shrewsbury. The traction requirements totalled 239 diesel-hydraulic locomotives comprising 150 Type 4, 69 Type 3, nine Type 2 and 11 Type 1, 71 of which had already been authorised as follows:

- 13 Type 3s were included in the batch approved in 1959 in advance of the submission of the final combined Areas 1 and 2 scheme, and were for use on routes excluded from the final scheme (see above and Table 8);
- 50 Type 3s had been approved in March 1960 for inclusion in the 1963 building programme in advance of the submission of the present scheme;
- 8 Type 2s were delivered for use in the original Area 1 and displaced as a result of amendments made to the scheme.

The design of the Type 1 was to be decided in consultation with the British Railways Central Staff. As regards the Type 4s, previously a cost of £135,000 per locomotive had been used, a figure that displeased the Commission, but Swindon now reckoned construction would cost £117,000.

Times were changing and, as will be seen in Chapter 12, MoT approval was now required for major expenditure. The WR had originally assessed its Type 1 requirement in terms of hundreds but the first part of the South Wales scheme sought only 11. Central Staff moves towards standardisation had brought forth a new 2,750hp diesel-electric specification that was likely to cost less than Swindon's 2,700hp diesel-hydraulic. With no cost advantage in favour of diesel-hydraulic, and with the weight of the two designs comparable, there was no reason to accede to the WR's request for 150 diesel-hydraulic Type 4s, and the 74 built for Area 2 represented the totality of the class.

A lower price for the diesel-hydraulic Type 3 over its diesel-electric equivalent won it approval. In 1963 Beyer Peacock, the contractor, enquired about the prospect of future orders in order to ensure continuity of production. Even at that date the WR told the Commission it would need an additional 400 examples, but across Areas 1, 2 and 3 eventual procurement totalled 101.

There is an intriguing entry in the Works Committee file for the meeting held on 29 November 1961. An agenda item concerning diesel-hydraulic traction involving John Ratter, the Committee chairman and (by then) a Commission Member, and WR representatives was never cleared for publication in the minutes. All that exists is a hand-written note to this effect from the meeting secretary! Whatever was discussed must have aroused acrimony because this is the only known such instance.

Finally, when Swindon got approval for its Type 1 diesel-hydraulic design, the number ordered was a mere 56. It was the only main line locomotive type built under the Modernisation Plan not to be mounted on bogies but instead had an 0-6-0 wheel arrangement. By the time the first examples appeared in 1964 it was already a white elephant because the duties for which it had been designed were disappearing rapidly.

None achieved a BR life of five years and some actually worked for a mere two! Although many were sold for use elsewhere, this still left the railways showing a significant loss. More modernisation money thrown away, but it did keep the metal bashers at Swindon occupied until 1965! The sales to industrial businesses then robbed private locomotive builders of potential orders.

Other Regional schemes

From the days of the Forms of Motive Power sub-committee in 1954, the ER held firm that 2,000hp diesels were inadequate for hauling inter-city services at average speeds of up to 75mph. In support, the Region calculated that to achieve a 70mph average between King's Cross and Retford without any recovery time for out-of-course delays, a locomotive of that power would have a load limit of only seven vehicles.

The ER was well provided for with Class 8P Pacifics that could, in the middle speed range and over limited distances, develop 2,000hp at the drawbar, not the rail or the engine or cylinders. Having lost out to the LMR in the main line electrification stakes, the advent of the 3,300hp EE prototype *Deltic* was viewed with interest.

Commission staff were divided on the suitability of this locomotive for East Coast express work, even though it was performing satisfactorily during service running on the LMR out of Euston. In July 1956 the Commission had made clear it judged that a single-unit diesel locomotive of between 3,000 to 3,500hp was required for non-electrified routes and work was under way on such a project.

As with all such matters, discussion went round and round, the Commission remarking in September 1957 that it was expecting a proposal from the Eastern Area Board. Supported by its East Coast partners, the NER and ScR, the ER sought authority for 23, later cut to 22, 'Deltic'-type locomotives. These were to replace 55 Pacifics but the scheme proposal surprisingly, perhaps craftily, used the Class A3 type as the engines to be phased out. At 30 years vintage, these were, of course, the oldest and least powerful of the East Coast Pacifics and there would have been a significantly lower capital write-off than if the 'A1s', built as late as 1948-9, had been withdrawn and so the financial case looked better.

The Commission commented positively in November, subject to safeguards, and agreed to the placing of a contract with EE on 20 February 1958, assuming agreement from the Eastern Area Board at the reduction to a fleet size of 22. Having already seen how the WR won out over BTC concern at the cost of its diesel-hydraulic programme, it was unsurprising that the East Coast partners did the same.

A five year guarantee period was provided and EE was contracted to carry out repairs and maintenance on the Deltic diesel engine. Delivery was to be as quickly as possible. Despite the forebodings, by October 1963 the performance of the small stud was one of very few bright spots in the diesel fleet, with most other classes suffering in one way or another.

On 26 June 1958 the Commission was asked to approve the ordering of an additional 70 Type 4s from EE as part of the 1959 building programme at an estimated cost of £6,090,000. Coming four months after the Type 5 'Deltic' order for the East Coast, Robertson expressed concern as to whether a 2,000hp locomotive was sufficiently powerful for the services for which they were to be used. He felt that heavy passenger trains travelling at high speeds needed greater power, but this type was too expensive to be used 'in tandem'. It was agreed to defer the order to enable the General Staff to consult with the Regions concerned.

The problem was that medium-speed diesel engines, such as EE's SVT and Sulzer's LDA28 ranges, developed insufficient horsepower per cylinder to provide a power unit of a size that could be fitted into a British locomotive that was capable of offering 3,000hp. General Motors diesels were, in fact, no better. The Deltic engines were quick-running and so produced more horsepower for the same overall mass, which is why two such power units could fit easily into a locomotive capable of operating in Britain. In essence, the railways were being modernised with a fleet of diesels of equal power to a Class 7 steam locomotive, which left no scope to improve train service timings.

August had brought worsening news concerning the BTC's trading position and this gave rise to considerable consternation. The minutes record an 'urgent need to discuss the dire financial position of the BTC and what emergency measures could be taken to stop the drain on cash resources'. This was driving Commission thinking. There should have been a pause in dieselisation to both await technical improvements that were under way, which would raise horsepower per cylinder, and to allow the Pilot Scheme concept of proving trials for designs already ordered to be concluded.

The following month EE's quote for 20 Type 4s arrived and the Commission found the price had risen to £214,800. This extra 10% should have led to a revised costing for the Area scheme in question and its viability reassessed but the official files provide no evidence this was done and such under-costing happened many times, thereby reducing the economic benefit of modernisation.

Next, the relatively small quantity of diesels required by the SR is worth reviewing because quoting from the BTC papers provides a flavour of how such matters were handled. A total of 98 Type 3s had been identified by the Region as its requirement and two batches totalling 65 had been ordered from BRCW for the first phase of the Kent Coast electrification. By 1959 consideration was being given to a further batch and tenders had been called for from contractors as set out in Table 9.

Table 9 Tenders for second batch of Type 3s for SR

Contractor	Mechanical parts	Engine type Engine hp	Electrical	Cost £	Bogies
Brush	Brush	Mirrlees JVSS 1,600hp	Brush	87,650	A1A-A1A
		Sulzer LDA28 1,550hp		94,850	
		Maybach MD865 1,535hp		81,550	Bo-Bo
BRCW	BRCW	Sulzer LDA28 1,550hp	Crompton Parkinson	78,940	Bo-Bo
EE	EE	18 cyl Deltic 1,700hp	EE	88,299	Bo-Bo
Metrovick	Metro-Cammell	Sulzer LDA28 1,550hp	Metrovick	99,368	A1A-A1A
		Mirrlees JVSS 1,600hp		104,172	Co-Co
				92,291	A1A-A1A
		Paxman		96,978	Co-Co
		12YLXL 1,500hp		87,213	A1A-A1A
				103,588	Co-Co

The Central Staff paper of April 1959 dealing with the procurement states:

> For SR the electrification scheme was approved for 98 diesel locomotives. The first 45 were included in the 1958 building programme and the order was placed with BRCW for 45 Type 3.
>
> The next 20 forms part of the 1960 building programme, and an order was placed with the same firm for 20 locomotives identical with the previous 45. Delivery of the first locomotive has been promised for November 1959 with completion of the total of 65 in February 1961.

A further 33 are to be ordered to complete the original approval of 98. Twelve of these are to conform to the Hastings gauge – which restricts the width of the locomotive. All 33 are to be available for service by early 1962.

As 65 of the 98 are BRCW design and build, it is logical for the remaining 33 to be of the same design. It is proposed the order should be placed with BRCW. The contract price for 20 ordered is £78,940. If BRCW got the order for the remaining 33, the price reduction for the 20 would work out at £78,380 and supply all 53 at this price, thereby saving £11,200 on the first 20, or £29,680 if assessed over the 53. The price excludes modifications to the 12 for the Hastings gauge, which involve over 100 new drawings, bogies, brake cylinders, sandboxes, driver's steps etc.

All 98 to be delivered by late summer 1961. In June 1958 when all manufacturers tendered, BRCW was the lowest at £78,940 for 20. Recommendation for the 33 Type 3s at £2,569,816. Forty two steam locomotives to be broken up.

This shows that BRCW was not just awarded the order on the basis of supplying the previous 65. It is also revealing as to which contractors submitted bids and the type of equipment proposed. For example, the Brush proposal for a Maybach engine was because the company was part of the same group as the UK licensee for the German marque. Note also that Metrovick joined forces with Metro-Cammell, whereas it was collaborating with Beyer Peacock on the building of 20 Type 2s as part of the Pilot Scheme.

Modern traction, steam era practices
The Regions were encouraged to convert to modern motive power on an area basis in order to eliminate steam from that area and avoid operating both types of traction side-by-side. Whilst this was laudable in one respect, it was merely putting 'new wine into old skins' to use the Biblical metaphor.

Most steam locomotives had diagrams that kept them close to their home depot, express passenger duties being the only real exception. By contrast, diesel and electric power could work long distances on daily rosters that could be for virtually the whole 24 hours. Sadly, thinking on motive power modernisation was in terms of the way steam had been utilised, rather than how the advent of the diesel might enable a more efficient regime to be brought in.

A good example concerns Blaydon shed on the NER. West of Newcastle-upon-Tyne, this small establishment covered local passenger and freight and was one of the first area schemes put forward by the Region. In November 1957 the requirement for 22 Type 4s to replace 41 steam locomotives was considered.

The previous month, Chairman Robertson and John Ratter, the Technical Adviser on the General Staff, had made an extensive tour of North American railways. These were organised with a few large centres of engineering and operating activity, rather than having the plethora of establishments that history had bequeathed to British Railways.

Henceforth Robertson wanted Regions to emulate American practice, with the existing motive power maintenance network replaced under modernisation with fewer bases in strategic locations. Robertson also reported that the introduction of diesels had seen a 40% reduction in maintenance and workshop staff in North America. Yet again, it was a measure of the ability of railway managers that it took a retired army general to point this out! The Blaydon scheme died and a new depot for the whole of Tyneside was created at Gateshead instead.

Even at this date – November 1957 – there was concern by Members that diesel utilisation was merely emulating steam, rather than taking advantage of its potential for greater availability. The Commission commented that it would reject schemes based on unacceptably low average miles per locomotive.

It was not only the way the Regions wanted to dieselise that began to be scrutinised more carefully at Commission level but also the traction they applied for. This has been seen with WR diesel-hydraulic building and also appertained when the ScR sought 12 of the new standard BR/Brush Type 4s in May 1961 for passenger and freight working in the Edinburgh and Glasgow areas.

Six locomotives were to be based at Haymarket depot for working heavy Anglo-Scottish services between Glasgow Queen Street and Edinburgh Waverley. The other six were to be based at Polmadie for heavy iron ore traffic in the Glasgow area and passenger diagrams from Glasgow to Birmingham, Manchester and Liverpool. The design was to be the same as proposed by the LMR for London to Glasgow and Perth north of Crewe. Of the forecast annual mileage of 1.1 million, 17% would be on freight turns, two machines were to be maintenance spares and 20 steam locomotives were to be condemned. The estimated cost was £1.2 million.

This highlights again that Regional planning was still built around prevailing operating practices, not those appropriate for a modern railway. There was no need to change diesels arriving in Edinburgh on Anglo-Scottish services for the final leg of their journey to Glasgow, as was the practice with steam traction. Small allocations of diesels were inefficient and, whilst West Coast Anglo-

Scottish traffic might have been shared between LMR and Polmadie depots in steam days, there was no need for this on a nationalised and modernised railway. The solution was to allocate all West Coast Anglo-Scottish traction at Crewe. As to the heavy mineral traffic, the ScR had to make do with less powerful types.

Diesel vs electric traction

In 1959 the BTC commissioned a firm of consulting engineers to opine on the balance of advantage as regards the two forms of traction. The firm failed to find an overseas model on which to base an assessment, presumably because no railway ran both forms on the same routes. It also included many caveats as to its conclusions. These included traffic density, the required rate of return on the capital invested and the extent to which electrification was just one part of route upgrading. Eventually the consultants came up with a figure of 200 miles as the break-even route mileage for the adoption of one or other system and this was for hauled trains, as opposed to multiple-unit stock.

Motive power headaches

The British locomotive industry saw the Modernisation Plan as its salvation and key to opening up overseas markets that had previously been supplied with steam power; how wrong could they be? Cox maintains that the re-ordering of a plethora of designs, rather than one standard type in each power class, was due to pressure from the railway industry, which wanted a home market showcase for each company's products. This approach cost the BTC millions, not just in first cost but in the need for an expanded range of spares, staff training and inferior productivity from 'dud' products.

Arguing against Cox's line, he overlooks the stated preference for the Brush Type 2 over the BRCW equivalent and this was why the latter were displaced as more of the former arrived. It does, at times, seem that Cox tries to deflect any criticism for decisions made during modernisation away from him and his engineering colleagues.

Steam locomotive construction was, essentially, metal bashing but diesel and electric traction was much more complicated, requiring completely different design principles. Companies such as NBL and Beyer Peacock found it hard to make the transition and went out of business. Robert Stephenson & Hawthorn had been acquired by EE but suffered a similar fate as no orders could be secured to keep it trading. Vulcan Foundry, also acquired by EE, fared better and turned its hands successfully to modern traction construction on the back of orders won by its parent, whose diesel engines and electrical equipment it installed but did not manufacture at the time. BRCW had struggled to meet delivery dates for the substantial locomotive and rolling stock orders it won from the BTC but these began to dry up by 1962. These metal bashers had gone by 1965.

NBL's liquidation left British Railways in an awkward position regarding the supply of Voith torque converters that were being built under licence for the WR's 2,700hp diesel-hydraulics. Eventually Voith took over part of one of NBL's workshops and fulfilled the contract requirements.

The problem was that overseas steam orders had generally come from countries in the British Empire and this was dissolving by 1960. These countries were by no means favourably disposed to their former master, whilst the scale of production that General Motors of the USA was able to achieve made its products significantly cheaper than those of British manufacturers. Not only did diesels and electrics built for British Railways modernisation not prove to be a springboard for overseas success, virtually no such business was actually secured and the locomotive industry in this country shrank to tiny, specialist proportions by 1970.

Companies like Paxman and Ruston – by then part of a merged GEC and EE – and Mirrlees – itself part of the same group as Brush – continued to develop and manufacture engines suitable for rail traction but these formed only part of their product ranges. The same was true for Brush and GEC as regards electrical equipment. Here was the rump of the private locomotive industry at the start of the 1970s.

Meanwhile, the Commission had to deal with the outwash from its hasty decision to order unproven, let alone untried, designs. NBL's Type 4 No D600 had suffered an embarrassing engine failure during its press run whilst returning from Bristol to Paddington on 17 February 1958, having been accepted into traffic three weeks earlier.

NBL's Type 2 designs fared worse, particularly the diesel-electric variant. Six diesel-hydraulic examples had been ordered as part of the assessment of that type of transmission and 10 further units added to the Pilot Scheme but with electric transmission to serve as a comparison. By 1959 NBL had secured further orders to bring each variant up to a fleet of 58 and deliveries were proceeding rapidly but not without problems.

At its meeting on 23 July the Commission noted the unsatisfactory performance of the locomotives, which was blamed on sub-standard workmanship, and no further orders were to be placed. On 26 November Robertson instructed Ratter to consider the premature condemnation of these, and other diesel locomotives whose performance was unsatisfactory and unlikely to improve. He was concerned not just about the timekeeping of the trains, but the excessive maintenance work and spares needed to keep them in traffic. Did he know that such a withdrawal programme would entail writing off nearly £7 million and that not all 116 NBL Type 2s had yet been built?

Nos D6100-37 of the diesel-electric class were allocated from new to London area ER sheds but the technical issues meant the Region wanted shot of them and in 1960 they were put to store in New England Yard, Peterborough. Despite being sheeted over, a diligent journalist caused a furore when he revealed that millions of pounds-worth of brand new diesels were dumped out of use.

The timing of the story could not have been worse because the BTC, and in particular its Modernisation Plan, was under intense Government scrutiny. All the locomotives went back to Scotland, where the 58 diesel-electrics became based, in order to be close to NBL's works for a range of modifications, not just to the engines but also to unsatisfactory GEC electrical equipment. Using this, and its diesel-hydraulic equivalents, to compare the two forms of transmission never got off the ground but this was no fault of the diesel-hydraulic type, which reports suggest fared much better on the WR.

Locomotive reliability became an additional running sore for the Commission on top of the ballooning size of its deficit and decreasing train punctuality. The engineers, predominantly on the mechanical side, felt Commission wrath. In addition to those affecting the NBL Type 2s already covered, during the first half of the 1960s the following represented a flavour of the technical issues.

Steam heating generator unreliability caused locomotives to be sidelined during the winter timetable.

Sulzer LDA28 12-cylinder engines experienced problems, notably the 'C' marque which had to be derated and returned to the manufacturer for rebalancing due to stress fracturing, with over 500 units involved including spares.

The Mirrlees engine in Brush Type 2s (approximately 270 units including spares) suffered stress failures and were replaced by an EE engine.

EE Type 2s required full engine rebuilds and other locomotive refurbishment.

Type 4 diesel-hydraulics of KMmechanical design (Classes 42, 43 and 52, totalling 145 locomotives) required modifications to bogies due to very poor riding.

The engineers carried out research on several engine types, as well as funding research by the private sector.

Traction planning
In March 1963 the British Railways Board (BRB) began to view the railways

as a single unit for planning purposes, a mere 15 years after nationalisation! Part of this was to be derived from a national traction plan for the main line diesels, which was to provide the basis on which better fleet utilisation could be planned. The Board then viewed the next step as the evolution of an efficient and economic basic timetable with provision for seasonal and variable traffic, compiled under central direction by a team representative of headquarters and the Regions.

Diesel locomotive performance generally continued to cause concern, as this extract from a Board minute of 15 May 1964 illustrates. The topic was the reduced locomotive availability caused by the failure of train heating generators, the decision to continue to use steam having been taken by the Technical Committee in 1955. The incidence of failures had not improved even with the modified boilers, and a fresh technical study was called for into the feasibility of the complete abolition of steam heating from BR rolling stock.

A past study had been inhibited by the expense involved in the conversion to electric train heating, but this would not weigh so heavily when applied to the smaller passenger fleet in future. So more wasted money and further expense in the conversion of traction and rolling stock was now to be the familiar outcome of flawed decision-making in the 1950s.

Two months later the new British Railways Board discussed operating performance. Figures for the past year pointed to a generally poor overall operating result. In particular, punctuality was unsatisfactory both for passenger and freight and that of the 'customer' trains in particular was described as disturbing.

Use of diesel locomotives and multiple-units did not show the rate of improvement that was desired because reliability was still unacceptably substandard. Reports on rolling stock showed the same general picture. Even the figures for the average miles per driver per day were low, so no wonder railway financial performance was still dreadful.

Substantially fewer locomotives were being diagrammed than were available and a large number of diagrams were not being worked by the appropriate locomotives. This unsatisfactory position was being discussed with the Regional Managers and steps would be taken to improve it with the introduction of the winter timetables, and targets would be set for 1965. Regional revenue budgets would also be used for focussing the need for such improvements.

It was to be 1965 before the national traction plan became a reality and Regions were expected to offer up surplus locomotives for reallocation. The first significant declared surplus were 20 of the 33 NBL-built 'V200s' (Class 43) but no other Region wanted them. Not long afterwards the WR offered up half of its brand-new Type 1s and, surprisingly, half were taken for local workings around Hull.

In 1967 the BR CM&EE produced two reports on the state of play of the main line diesel fleet. The first dealt with what were described as, the major types – Classes 17, 20, 24, 25, 31, 33, 35, 37, 40, 44-6, 47, 52 and 55 – and the minor classes – Classes 14-16, 21-3, 26-9, 41-3 – were covered in the second. Both were technical states of play, highlighting issues that affected performance and how these should be tackled. Only the EE-built designs were up to scratch and considerable sums were either being lost by poor availability requiring a bigger fleet or in terms of remedial work. Decide in haste, repent at leisure – and at what cost!

To round off the story of the dieselisation of Britain's railways, Table 10 (overleaf)sets out the deliveries by class and by year. On 11 August 1968 main line steam traction on service trains ended, yet the Modernisation Plan had forecast there would still be over 7,000 locomotives of this type in traffic then. The forecast number of diesels proved to be wildly exaggerated, probably because of a lack of understanding of the potential of modern motive power.

Back in 1954 there were around 19,000 steam locomotives. By 1968 there were 3,100 main line diesels, around 4,000 DMU vehicles (the vast majority formed into two-, three- or four-car sets) and 2,000 shunters, of which 1,700 had been built after 1954. Of course the railway network had shrunk during this period from 19,000 to 12,000 miles, a near 40% cut.

By 1978, all the Derby lightweight DMUs and all the diesel-hydraulics had gone and the national traction plan was wrestling with an ageing fleet, bought over quite a short period, which needed either replacement or significant expenditure to maintain some semblance of reliable performance. It was to take until the new Millennium and rail privatisation for the outwash from the modernisation of motive power to be finally dealt with in terms of a second fleet renewal.

Table 10 Main line diesel deliveries 1957 to 1968

TOPS Class	1957	1958	1959	1960	1961	1962
14	-	-	-	-	-	-
15	1	9	8	21	5	-
16	-	10	-	-	-	-
17	-	-	-	-	-	14
20	16	4	26	4	60	18
21	-	3	35	20	-	-
22	-	-	8	27	2	21
23	-	-	10	-	-	-
24, 25	-	5	56	87	23	5
26, 27	-	10	37	-	19	50
28	-	8	12	-	-	-
30	3	17	58	103	48	34
33	-	-	-	38	45	15
35	-	-	-	-	16	48
37	-	-	-	4	28	62
40	-	10	44	64	54	28
41	-	4	1	-	-	-
42, 43	-	3	11	25	25	7
44, 45, 46	-	-	9	27	96	55
47	-	-	-	-	-	4
50	-	-	-	-	-	-
52	-	-	-	-	1	28
55	-	-	-	-	20	2
Total	20	83	315	420	442	391

1963	1964	1965	1966	1967	1968	Total
-	25	31	-	-	-	56
-	-	-	-	-	-	44
-	-	-	-	-	-	10
53	50*	-	-	-	-	117
-	-	-	57	40	3	228
-	-	-	-	-	-	58
-	-	-	-	-	-	58
-	-	-	-	-	-	10
78	95	64	54	11	-	477
-	-	-	-	-	-	116
-	-	-	-	-	-	20
-	-	-	-	-	-	263
-	-	-	-	-	-	98
34	3	-	-	-	-	101
106	52	57	-	-	-	309
-	-	-	-	-	-	200
-	-	-	-	-	-	5
-	-	-	-	-	-	71
6	-	-	-	-	-	193
63	186	193	57	8	1	512
-	-	-	-	3	47	50
40	5	-	-	-	-	74
-	-	-	-	-	-	22
380	416	345	168	62	51	3,093

Chapter 11

Modernisation of train services

Passenger services

At its meeting on 17 March 1955, the Commission discussed the compilation of a traffic survey, which would deal with traffic problems in the broadest sense. This issue had been indicated by the industrialist and part-time Commission Member H. P. Barker, and needed to be resolved before certain large-scale projects could satisfactorily be undertaken.

Arising from this, on 26 July 1956, the Commission considered documents appertaining to passenger traffic policy from the Traffic Survey Group (dated March 1956) and memoranda dated 20 July on the study produced by the General Staff, which also covered traction policy. These were described as purely staff papers and it was to be left to the six Area Boards to use these when planning Regional projects.

Headings under which Regions were to plan comprised:

- Traction – locomotives and multiple units, diesel or electrification schemes;
- Timetable – pattern, frequency and speed, 70 to 75mph being the express yardstick average, dependent on the number of stops;
- Categories – Pullman, special expresses to meet Regional requirements and ordinary expresses;
- Utilisation of staff and stock;
- Amenities;
- Coaching stock design, including addressing poor ride quality;
- Dealing with peak traffic;
- Terminal station facilities.

It was at this meeting that the Commission pretty much abandoned the Pilot Scheme by saying requests for additional diesels would be considered.

In April 1957, the proposals of the Area Boards were compiled in a massive document entitled 'Report on diesel and electric traction and the passenger services of the future based on proposals of the Area Boards'.

By now, 444 diesels and 2,741 DMU vehicles had been ordered and the General Staff promised to expedite the progress of further submissions in order to modernise motive power as rapidly as possible by 1962. Whilst the Commission would give 'in principle' decisions, final sanction would be dependent on a detailed and economically-justified case.

Proposals within the report envisaged an additional 2,750 gangwayed, hauled-coaches in addition to the 1,750 already on order. The total of 1,369 EMU vehicles were to be bolstered by 1,200. DMU vehicles of all types were to increase by 2,395 beyond the existing 274, plus an unspecified number of long-distance DMUs of a new design for the East Coast line.

Passenger station upgrading, where the cost would exceed £50,000, had identified 50 sites. Remarkably, only Euston on the planned West Coast electrification scheme was excluded from the major stations and this oversight caused embarrassment when extra funds for its rebuilding had to be sought!

Additional electrification schemes beyond 1963 envisaged both East and West Coast lines through to Aberdeen, Midland Lines routes to Manchester and Leeds and the Southern route to Exeter and Weymouth, all at 25kV. A survey was in progress concerning electrification between Paddington and South Wales.

A few points made by several Regions are worthy of note.

The SR eschewed diesel railbuses because the economies appeared too marginal and lacked flexibility for the planned-for patronage growth. Service planning would be around 'reasonably good', rather than 'spectacularly fast' trains because of the extra track capacity required for the latter. A frequent, regular-interval pattern was to be the hallmark in timetable planning. Attaining overall average speeds of 75mph was not seen to be practical. Multiple-units were preferred to hauled trainsets for the ease of terminal turnrounds and splitting portions at junctions. This view excluded the Waterloo to Exeter and Weymouth routes, where further consideration was needed.

The Southern Area Board disagreed with its Regional Manager concerning coaching stock, where the latter favoured seating in compartments, whilst the former favoured research on carriage interior design and passenger comfort. Another aspect that brought disagreement was over whether to redevelop the London termini. The Area Board saw this as offering potential for better facilities, whereas the Regional Manager felt any work wouldn't be worth the expected high cost.

Despite the ScR Regional Manager professing disinterest in diesel traction during the planning of the Modernisation Plan in 1954, by 1959 the Region had seen railbuses as the saviour of loss-making lines instead of discussing alternative bus services with other parts of the Commission. The Region also had plans for the dieselisation of services over the Highland and Great North of Scotland routes by 1963.

By that date, the LMR assessed that express passenger trains from St Pancras to Leeds and Manchester, together with those along the North East/South West Corridor to Bristol, would have diesel traction. Of course this implied continuation of the pre-nationalisation boundary, which saw trains from the North East and Midlands over LMSR metals terminate there, except for holiday extras at weekends. It was to take until the 1970s for a complete recast of the North to South West timetable, with through running of trains, in a manner that should have been tackled after nationalisation.

A digression here into West Coast electrification is appropriate. In 1956 this scheme from Euston to Birmingham, Liverpool and Manchester had been estimated at £118 million and a financial impact assessment was sought by the Commission in 1957 when the Crewe to Manchester section was authorised; this took two years to produce. A new price tag of £159.8 million was attached, £113 million being the 'betterment' after stripping out costs of maintaining the route without electrification. The original estimate seems to have allowed insufficient for rebuilding structures to give the necessary clearances and there was talk of adopting 6.25kV at certain locations.

A net return of 7% on the investment for the scheme was lower than a diesel alternative, which was calculated at 10%. Electric traction was expected to generate higher revenues, partly because faster timings would be possible with a locomotive capable of over 3,000hp at the rail, when compared to 2,000hp from a heavier 2,500hp (gross) diesel. Substituting 3,300hp 'Deltics' cut the return on a diesel scheme to 8% and having already committed well in excess of £10 million on Crewe to Manchester and the order for 100 locomotives, the clear choice was electrification.

The LMR's report omitted to include the cost of interest on capital borrowed during the project before the new assets began earning revenue, possibly over £10 million. A poorly-expounded case fell foul of the Parliamentary Committee on the Nationalised Industries in its 1960 review of railway modernisation. Commission Member Barker considered that estimates of the amount of equipment, including diesel locomotives, needed was excessive and that the appraisal merely grafted new facilities onto existing practices.

In the face of criticism, all the Commission could do was to claim that experience worldwide showed electrification schemes habitually over-performed estimates of traffic. Even Prime Minister Harold MacMillan proffered his opinion that a fleet of modern steam locomotives was the best way forward! Strangely, the Commission failed to use the data from the report it had initiated from external consultants on the relative merits of diesel and electric traction in terms of traffic density.

Further Government scrutiny brought a fresh internal review and this cut the net project cost to £153 million; one factor in the change was the inclusion of traffic not originating on the route. It now seems bizarre that this was excluded originally and one wonders whether workings north and also west of Crewe fell into this category because they originated off the routes to be electrified! An alternative diesel scheme showed no better return this time, caused by revising the cost of a diesel locomotive from £100,000 (an EE Type 4 in 1958 but certainly well below the BR/Sulzer 2,500hp Type 4) to an average of £138,000 by including a quantity of 'Deltics' at an estimated £150,000 each.

After quite some deliberation, the Minister gave his approval on 31 January 1961 to an agreed total spend, including station improvements, of £175 million. No information on the final cost has been unearthed but, by dint of economies such as excluding some lines, there is evidence to suggest there was no further cost over-run.

It took until October 1962 for the redevelopment of Euston station to be signed off. The final cost was close to £16 million, the provision of a hotel being dropped because of a lack of money, while arguments about the price were still active in BR committees into 1968.

Service patterns and speed
By 1966 modern traction provision on the West and East Coast routes and on the WR had enabled progress towards a timetable based on clock-face departures, usually with a set pattern of intermediate stops, a practice long-established on the SR.

One of the three types of express passenger train proposed by the General Staff paper in 1956 was the 'special', something distinctive above and beyond the ordinary expresses. The ER ran fast, limited-stop services aimed at the business market such as the 'West Riding' from Leeds to King's Cross which only called at Wakefield. When Gerry Fiennes, a keen advocate of the Class 55 'Deltics' for the East Coast, became the General Manager (as Regional Managers had gradually become known) of the WR he tried to borrow an example for trials on his Region. Request denied, he turned instead to the use of pairs of Class 37s, passed for 100mph, which were used with two rakes of coaches to operate special expresses from 1965 from Paddington to Bristol and Swansea.

Modern traction brought across-the-board progress in train timings. Well into the 1960s, the first northbound Euston to Glasgow service was the 'Royal Scot' at around 10.00 and most through trains ran overnight because of the length of journey. Inauguration of regular electrically-hauled trains into Euston on 22 November 1965 was a key factor in shortening timings and gradually moving from night to day-time travel. Across the network as a whole, in 1970 many services were achieving average speeds of 70mph or over during at least part of their journey. Prewar, 115 trains were timed at just 60mph.

The time-honoured practice of serving places with a through coach, detached en route, went into severe decline. Even so, this was not always bad news; for example, Cromer no longer had a through coach from London but modernised services in Norfolk meant a shorter journey time could be achieved by changing at Norwich.

One aspect of modernisation that was completely overlooked was the promotion of expresses. Railway posters focused on sunny seaside scenes or jolly places of interest but without a clear link to how a modern express would whisk you there in comfort and convenience. Rival salesmen extolled the benefits of visiting such places once you bought a car from them. Railway timetables of the period were presented, seemingly, for the aficionado, not a mere member of the public.

During the 1960s there was a sea-change, albeit slow, towards advertising directed to the non-rail traveller. This can be demonstrated by the image of a businessman on a Manchester 'Blue Pullman', skimming through suburbia at high speed whilst enjoying refreshments and reading papers for his forthcoming meeting. Whilst commercially a flop for reasons explained elsewhere, this form of advertising ensured loadings were high.

Freight services

Freight traffic can usefully be divided between merchandise and container activity, sundries (smaller than a complete wagonload), being part of the former. Under Chairman Beeching's stewardship, during the mid-1960s the concept of the trainload – an entire train of goods being conveyed for a single client – was developed.

The Plan earmarked £365 million for freight facilities, rolling stock and associated equipment. An equivalent to the planning document of July 1956 sketching out Commission thinking on passenger services of the future was not produced for freight activity. Whether this was a contributory factor in some of the decisions taken is a moot point.

Merchandise network facilities

£80 million had been included in the Plan for the construction and reconstruction of 55 marshalling yards, which would result in the total or partial closure of about 150 existing facilities. For example, at Carlisle Kingmoor a new yard was to replace eight smaller ones. Its location was at the confluence of four routes from the south and three from the north, surely a vital location for the interchange of traffic? The ScR had the worst existing setup, with over 80 yards from its pre-Grouping inheritance, with consequential duplication.

By 1962 marshalling yards had been, or were being built at Perth, Thornton Junction (Fife), Millerhill (Edinburgh), Kingmoor (Carlisle), Tyne (Lamesley), Tees (Thornaby), Margam (Port Talbot), Healey Mills (Wakefield), Tinsley (Sheffield), Ripple Lane (Barking), Temple Mills (Stratford, East London) and Ashford (Kent). The report on the Reshaping of British Railways (the Beeching report) in 1963 halted work on yards still to be built because they were seen as very expensive and out of line with a modern freight policy.

Modern yards were more efficient than tripping wagons between several local, pre-Grouping, equivalents but they still did not make the traffic pay. Freight that moved from loading to unloading without interruption was profitable, whereas any break in the transit – goods depot or marshalling yard – made a loss.

International traffic was not overlooked within the Plan, with improved cargo-handling facilities at several ports, including Holyhead and Heysham. Upgraded facilities for Continental traffic were provided at Hither Green and Bricklayers Arms.

General merchandise traffic was to be concentrated at depots equipped with modern handling equipment, such as fork lift trucks for loading cargo into the new pallet vans. The LMR planned to reduce the number of such depots from 170 to fewer than 50, whilst in the Plymouth area a new depot at Friary dealt with all the merchandise traffic for both the Southern and Western Regions. Official photographs proudly depicting modernised goods depots showed men 'hand-balling' (picking up, moving and putting down) items of goods from wagon interiors onto fork-lift trucks, providing yet another instance of old operating practices with new equipment. There was no way such an operation could ever pay!

Cross-London freight movements had been an operational difficulty for years, not least by requiring crews at London sheds where recruitment was very difficult. As part of a solution, a scheme was devised for a London orbital freight route from Redhill via Reading, Oxford, Bletchley to Bedford. A marshalling yard was to be built at Swanbourne, west of Bletchley, and a flyover was constructed at Bletchley to avoid conflicting moves across the West Coast line.

The scheme had a price tag of £11.7 million in 1959 but was recognised as 'never expected to show a direct financial return'. It was abandoned in 1960 and serves as a good example of railway managers solving yesterday's problems instead of looking towards future opportunities. The Bletchley flyover was already being built by then at a cost of £1.6 million. Without this facility, however, it would have been virtually impossible to bring passenger and freight trains from the Oxford direction across the main line because of the speed and density of the inter-city services.

Despite the vast sums poured into modernising the merchandise freight operation, there is no evidence that it actually ever paid its way. As the 1960s turned into the 1970s, more and more depots closed, a notable example being that at Huskisson, which served Liverpool's north docks and which had been modernised but which closed in 1976.

A year earlier, BR launched a revamped merchandise network, known as Speedlink, which used air-braked wagons – note, not vacuum-braked as per the Plan! When railborne freight was forced by Government to be financially viable in the 1980s, and the freight business was divided into different business units called sectors, it became clear that such traffic could not be viable and the Speedlink service ended in 1991.

Just how great was the mistaken belief of railway managers that this traffic could ever be made viable will never be known, but no transport undertaking in the private sector could have survived such a trading model. Bear in mind that the railways never had any mandate to lose money on its freight activities and losses in one operation had to be covered by profits elsewhere.

Block and company trains

Having botched the first round of mineral wagon modernisation for reasons described below, it was the Reshaping report again which pointed the way forward. The concept of circuit (later called merry-go-round) working probably dates from 1960 but the obstacle was that the NCB, in particular, would not build at its expense the necessary facilities for loading and discharging trains in motion at very slow speed.

Eventually the stand off between BR and its clients was resolved. A new design of 45-ton gross, 32-ton capacity, disc- and air-braked two-axle wagons of basic French design and capable of running at 45mph full or 60mph empty was put in hand and revolutionised coal flows. After trials at West Burton Power Station, the six-mile circuit between Monktonhall Colliery and Cockenzie Power Station east of Edinburgh was the first full mgr operation when it began in 1966 and was planned around three 28-wagon consists making five daily round trips.

The 1963 Reshaping report can lay claim to being the freight traffic survey never carried out by the BTC because another innovation was the company train, though mgr circuits could rightly be dubbed NCB trains. In any event, the expanding motor industry took the opportunity to use rail for block shipments between factory and distribution head. For example, in 1965 the Ford plants at Dagenham and Halewood were sending a combined five trains each week to Bathgate, Scotland, five from each plant weekly to Wakefield and two daily from Dagenham to Garston, Liverpool.

Another innovation with Reshaping was the striking of long-term contracts with major clients and these often involved the client providing the rolling stock. By 1965 15 of the largest oil companies had signed such deals and the influence of retired oil executive, L. Williams, who joined the British Railways Board in 1963, in this is acknowledged. Although the tonnage of oil had grown by 150% between 1954 and 1962, BR's share had dropped to just 12½%; just what were the railway's commercial managers doing between those years to have overlooked this?

Bulk cement and aggregates for construction sites, particularly new roads, were other company flows developed during the 1960s. Gradually the track across the network was upgraded to permit higher axle-loads.

Container and inter-modal traffic
The transport of containers, in the broadest sense, by both road and rail was by no means a new concept in 1954. The use of tanks to transport beer, milk and a wide variety of other liquids on lorries and railway wagons was well established. During the planning stage of the Modernisation Plan, the Technical Committee began to examine the feasibility of 'roadrailers', whereby a road trailer would be loaded onto a railway wagon.

In 1960 a prototype vehicle called a roadrailer was built as a collaborative private/BR venture. It was markedly different from the original concept and was a road trailer with two sets of wheels – road and rail – which were raised or lowered by compressed air. Roadrailers were to couple together by means of a special connection and then be capable of being hauled by the use of a barrier vehicle, which would have a special coupling at one end and a conventional rail one at the other. Roadrailers avoided the need for terminals with overhead loading gantries and in February 1961 the Commission decided to allocate the 40 prototype vehicles to the ER but the concept never proved attractive.

The Technical Committee was also asked by the Commission to investigate flows that would be suitable for transport of small containers. In January 1955 the Chairman authorised an extra £5,000 on equipment for the transfer of containers from road to rail. Even by the start of 1961 the unresolved question was the size of the container.

The first dedicated container service was the 'Condor' (container door-to-door) between London Hendon and Gushetfaulds Glasgow. Using a pair of Type 2 diesels, a trial run was made on 1 October 1958 and the service was inaugurated the following spring, the 400-mile journey being timed for 10 hours. January 1963 witnessed a new northbound flow from Birmingham. Container size was smaller than the later standard at four tons capacity and two were carried on each bogie flat wagon; this size was perhaps a factor in why the service fizzled out when the larger, standard container arrived.

It was to be 1964 before decisions were taken on container and wagon design and on 24 June the BRB authorised 34 wagons and 252 containers in connection with proposed London-Glasgow liner train services as Route 1 of Stage 1 of a proposed container liner train network, London to Glasgow serving as the pilot. In advance of this, in March 1963 the Technical Committee accepted a recommendation that five examples of both Classes 40 and 47 should be equipped for train air braking. Retro-fitting most of the fleet over the next decade was to be a costly exercise caused by poor judgement in keeping faith with vacuum braking in 1955.

This was also the death knell for vacuum-braked rolling stock. It was also the dawn of the bogie wagon, capable of running at 75mph. In addition to container flat wagons, rolling stock of this kind was developed in different forms for the company trains referred to above.

Freight train braking

The decision to opt for the vacuum system of automatic continuous train braking, dates from the Grouping of the railways into the Big Four in 1923. Its advantages over air brakes were lower cost and the absence of patent issues.

The choice between the two systems was debated by the Technical Committee in March 1954, when a report from Central Staff officers reviewing options stated that air brakes on freight vehicles were slower to apply and release than vacuum.

Despite most American and Continental railways having chosen air, cost again won the day, not just because the system was cheaper to fit but its continued use would avoid the expense of dual braking. Another argument put forward was consistency with existing vehicle stock, though there were not many wagons so fitted in 1954.

Having decided on the vacuum system, retro-fitting the existing fleet was put at £75 million in the Plan but this had rocketed to £175 million by 1957; it was eventually halted in 1960. Another issue was that the system was not suited to long trains, which modern motive power could handle.

By then, the Commission had ordered 295,000 brake cylinders over a five-year period from Westinghouse at £23 each. Cancellation of the plan for vacuum brake-fitting the traditional type of mineral wagon fleet resulted in a claim from the company which was settled at £1.6 million. Other suppliers also brought claims for curtailed orders.

Nevertheless, between 1954 and 1962 the number of low-capacity wagons (under 14 tons) was reduced from 77% to 46% but average wagon capacity was still only 16.6 tons. Continuously-braked wagons increased from 166,000 to 320,000, whilst the total stock reduced from 1,107,000 to 849,000.

Having embarked on a large programme of mineral wagon modernisation as part of the Plan, the NCB and the British Iron & Steel Federation banned the new vehicles because the brake under-gear could foul their facilities, and sadly this was yet another example of bad planning by railway managers in not consulting clients.

A further issue was that having a mixed fleet of braked and unbraked merchandise vehicles meant that picking up and setting down those without brakes at wayside station goods yards or in private sidings meant the whole train would have to be worked as unbraked.

Commission Member Barker poured derision on the situation, arguing that the braking policy had rested on two unsound principles, 'that it was practicable to modernise the present fleet and implicitly that if this were done the economic ends would justify the means'.

Among the benefits expected of the Modernisation Plan were faster, more reliable freight services. It will therefore serve as a conclusion to this chapter to quote from a BRB minute of 25 February 1965 under the heading of 'Reliability Of Service':

> It is of paramount importance in the development of the long-term freight market, the policy to gain the full confidence of both trade and industry in reliability of the rail service. The present unreliable service, in many cases, inhibited potential customers from committing themselves to rail on any large scale. Further, there was

a real chance of hardening (raising) rates, particularly in the sundries field, if reliable service was the rule.

Ten years into the Plan, these objectives still seemed some way off!

Chapter 12

Modernisation reappraised

Financial failings

Railway modernisation cannot be discussed in isolation from the broader situation of the BTC, otherwise the context is missing.

The 1954 annual report, published in 1955 after Government approval for the Plan had been forthcoming, referred again to restrictions imposed by Government and resource availability on capital development within the Commission's activities since nationalisation in 1948. Such programmes that had been implemented had been confined to 'making good the serious arrears of replacement which were inherited' since the war.

The report continued that there had now been an easing of restrictions on capital expenditure that had inhibited technical betterment and the Commission was now in a better position to 'take a broader, bolder and longer-term view of the future role of British Railways'. Referring to the Plan itself, the report said that in its preparation it was 'necessary to ensure that the cost of modernisation was fully justified by the economies it was expected to bring and by the improved revenues to be earned from freight and passenger services which would be speeded up and made more reliable'. What could be done in a given period was recognised as being constrained by the constructional and manufacturing capabilities of the Commission and outside industry.

A series of events was, however, to lay bare the dire situation in which British Railways would find itself in the latter part of the 1950s and just where it did make and lose money. Even before then, in 1953 the Railway Executive's minutes make clear there was concern that the network was not fulfilling its obligation to break even as required under the Transport Act of 1947 and measures would be needed to address this.

First, the Government was fighting inflation and, inevitably, public utilities suffered price controls and British Railways came off the worst. When permission was forthcoming to raise rates, these were below the prevailing level of inflation and retrospective, the railways playing catch-up.

Secondly, 1957 and 1958 witnessed a significant drop in mineral traffic as a result of a fall-off in industrial production. This exposed the fragility of the railways' trading position because overall losses soared. It became apparent to some that only the mineral flows and parts of the inter-city passenger traffic were making any money; everything else was either loss-making or chronically so.

A clue had come from the 1953 traffic survey, which found that passenger services lost £60 million overall. Despite having had rates pegged below inflation, local railway commercial managers *cut* them in order to win more business that was already being carried at a loss; economies of scale did not apply here.

Thirdly, the trouble was that many, but not all, of the senior people in the BTC did not truly understand British Railways' situation. Critically, totally inadequate traffic costing methods meant managers had no accurate idea of which, if any, activities were profitable or how much others were losing money. There was a myopic belief that modernisation would make everything all right, barring some 'basket case' lines – some rural, some urban – that were proposed for closure.

No one (or insufficient people with influence) questioned whether modernising the merchandise 'sundries' traffic – the door-to-door collection and delivery service for consignments just too large to despatch via the postal service – would allow it to break even, let alone pay its way. Yet handling this, and parcels traffic, meant that all stations through which such traffic passed had to be fully manned. Modernisation might speed up transit times but not bring extra net financial value to the railways to pay for the investment. Blind faith was attached to the belief that a modern sundries business would win back traffic from the roads, and presumably pay its way.

By 1955 the 25-mile restriction on 'C' licence transport had been lifted. Businesses which owned commercial vehicles for the conveyance of their own goods required a Government licence – category 'C' – for each vehicle in order to operate on the roads. Category 'A' and 'B' licences appertained to vehicles used for hire and reward, in other words by transport undertakings whose business was the conveyance of the goods of other businesses. A 25-mile limit on how far 'C' licence vehicles could travel pushed sundries traffic to the railways but, with this removed, businesses could transport their own goods from door to door without restriction other than a maximum speed of 40mph on the vehicle. By contrast, using rail meant taking it to a depot and then having it moved from the receiving rail station to the customer.

No one in the BTC foresaw the rapid growth in 'C' licence vehicles during the second half of the 1950s and, to be fair, the changes in the pattern of transport over the 15 years of the Plan could not have been foreseen. Chairman Robertson had raised this issue with a trade body in February 1959 and wanted an enquiry into the circumstances.

By May the Commission had recognised that moving sundries and wagonload merchandise by rail was less convenient than by road but still believed it offered a cheaper alternative. This was despite the BTC holding the belief that road transportation was, effectively, subsidised. In considering competition from 'C' licence operators, A. R. Dunbar, the Manpower Adviser on the General Staff, felt that most manufacturers would not want the problems associated with running one or more road vehicles when they could use a modern rail carrier.

It's always easy to condemn with hindsight, but how wrong was BTC thinking! No volume of sundries business at competitive rates would ever have made it viable for the railways and this is not just the case in Britain but in virtually every country. In fact, the same is true even for general merchandise traffic of less than a wagonload delivered to a private siding.

The problem was twofold. First, and as the BTC acknowledged, rail was less convenient and over most distances could never be as quick as a single lorry going door-to-door. So the belief that modernised merchandise services would win back traffic was utterly wrong. Rail was better for bulk flows and for long hauls.

Then the BTC believed its modernised merchandise services would compete on price by cutting rates. This was thought without any idea of the cost of moving sundries and small merchandise consignments and also took no account of having to pay interest on the sums borrowed to fund modernisation.

Fourthly, in many ways the nationalised railways were still thinking in a localised mindset, without cross-boundary strategy. Even worse was that Regions competed between themselves to win freight traffic and refused to rationalise duplicate facilities. This can best be illustrated by squabbling between the LMR and WR in 1958.

Duplicate facilities existed in the West Midlands and the two Regions could not agree how to rationalise these. The issue dragged on during 1958 to the point of exasperation of the BTC Chairman and was settled by the bi-Regional arrangement being abolished and replaced by separate Regional establishments. A good illustration can be found in the WR's plans for diesel locomotive maintenance in the West Midlands, which involved the conversion of Wolverhampton Stafford Road Works into a major depot. This was abandoned in 1962 when the LMR gained control of routes north of Banbury and assigned the work to Crewe instead.

Another example of the impact of a lack of a central guiding hand can be seen in the 1958 marshalling yards panel's report. The BTC was so dissatisfied that it told the panel to come up with a comprehensive plan that was not tackling the matter on a Regional or individual yard basis. Factional elements also squabbled over future freight traffic patterns, some preferring conventional types of equipment, whilst others preferred something more revolutionary. Meanwhile, modernisation capital continued to be poured into new short-wheelbase wagons and terminals to load and unload them.

The tide only began to change around 1960. This can be illustrated in the planning of the Tinsley marshalling yard on a new site where connection from former competing railway companies' routes could be laid in to eliminate duplicate yards around the Greater Sheffield area.

Concurrently, Gerry Fiennes, the Commission's Chief Operating Officer, was put to work on closing the former Great Central route north of Aylesbury to Sheffield. This was not an LMR initiative, as is often claimed, and was assisted by the unforeseen rapid fall-off in coal shipments from Derbyshire and Nottinghamshire south along this route.

A significant spur towards long-overdue rationalisation came from the new Minister of Transport, Ernest Marples. Spending on modernisation schemes now had to receive his approval and a prerequisite was the closure of duplicate facilities. By way of example, the WR London to Wolverhampton passenger services were downgraded to semi-fast when the LMR's route out of Euston was electrified.

Fifthly, the cost/benefit analysis of many modernisation schemes appears amateurish. A good example can be found in the way Area dieselisation proposals were costed and thus justified but which were based on locomotive prices that were seriously below actual.

The Central Staff had a 'ready reckoner' of the price of locomotives in each power category. The railway workshops used these, rather than having the sort of costing systems that were essential for outside contractors and, in truth, no one really knew, or cared, how much it cost British Railways to build a locomotive; it was assumed it would be lower than a contractor but this appears to be the opposite of the true situation.

Dieselisation by area was based on these assumed locomotive prices but they were quickly found to be well wide of the mark. Take, for instance, the NBL Type 2 diesel-hydraulics. The six ordered under the Pilot Scheme had cost £53,000 each but when the WR wanted 52 more in 1957 for its Area 1 scheme, NBL upped the price by £10,800. NBL argued that the original quote had been given in 1953 and was no longer valid in June 1957 and the Central Staff expressed concern as to how this 20% hike would affect Area 1's viability but did nothing further to investigate the matter – money no object!

Reviews of the Modernisation Plan

The BTC had to, basically, break even; there was no Government subsidy provision. By the end of 1955, however, an accumulated deficit of £70 million had arisen. External concern emerged as early as 1956 about BTC finances when the Minister of Transport sought a detailed review and a White Paper was published in October. This presented a state of play and forward look across all activities. The Commission forecast it would be paying its way by 1961/2, provided it could continue to modernise; provided it could adjust rates in line with cost rises; provided it could modify its services as it thought best. By now, the cost of modernisation had risen to £1,660,000.

The Commission foresaw that it was during this period (1957-1962) that the most striking developments in the Plan must be achieved. The period beyond 1962 was seen as one of sustained development and gradual transition to electric traction.

As regards traction, the first objective was to obtain in the least possible time the maximum benefit that could be derived from the use of diesel motive power in all its forms. The second was to carry through a programme of electrification as fast as circumstances would permit which would continue until all the main trunk lines and such others as could be justified were electrified, using diesel traction for the rest.

Concerning the elimination of steam, in January 1957 the Commission expected steam to have been replaced on all suburban and branch line services by 1961 or the facilities withdrawn.

The White Paper provided some interesting statistics and among these was the impact of introducing DMUs. On services from Birmingham New Street to Lichfield, takings had risen by 208%, whilst between Bury and Bacup the growth had been 164%. Not so good was growth of 44% along the former Midland & Great Northern route between Kings Lynn, Wells and Norwich which had been 30%. Of course takings were not profits and on 22 May 1958 the Commission sanctioned a staged closure of this line, commencing in 1959. Modernisation was not the sole answer to Commission losses; as a commentator had written in 1955, it merely made the inefficiency chromium-plated!

Hard economic times were a significant factor in railway freight traffic volumes but the Government also sought to curb funds for Modernisation Plan projects in 1957 and 1958. This forced the Commission to carry out a reassessment of schemes in order to see which offered the best prospect for quick pay-backs by 1962, others being postponed. The LMR moaned that no alternative provision for diesel traction had been made for the Crewe to Manchester route; the ER claimed potential operating difficulties if conversion of the Liverpool Street, Chelmsford and Southend line to 25kV AC was held up; the ScR explained the difficulties that would ensue if Stage 1 of the Glasgow suburban electrification was suspended.

Reading the BTC minutes one gets a feeling of near-panic as losses mounted year by year and this situation drove Commission thinking above all other considerations. It also prompted fresh Parliamentary attention on the worth of the vast sums being spent on modernisation as the economy worsened. First off the blocks was the Government and then came the Select Committee on the Nationalised Industries.

As early as October 1958 Chairman Robertson was emphasising the need to complete the West Coast electrification project as soon as possible to obtain the benefits. He also wanted ER and WR dieselisation schemes pushed ahead.

With an accumulated deficit of around £270 million, in 1959 the Modernisation Plan was reappraised again, a second White Paper published in July and then debated in Parliament. On 29 January the Commission discussed the reappraisal against the background of deteriorating finances. The Regional Managers were to be consulted later that day with the intention of hastening completion of projects to which the BTC was already fully committed and re-ordering priorities on others.

One issue now emerging was whether the BTC would ever be able to clear its deficit, on which interest was accruing, and if this could not be done, then there would have to be a writing-off of at least part of the debt, which would amount to a retrospective subsidy. Concomitant with this was the worry that this would embed inefficiency in the organisation.

Was this a fair view among Parliamentarians? Previous chapters have brought out instances of inefficiencies in procurement during modernisation. Some Regions were markedly less keen to consider service withdrawals and line closures than others. With no commercial board of directors on the back of the Regional Managers to ensure the railway was not run at a loss, it is easy to form the impression that Regions had turned into personal fiefdoms for some of the Regional Managers.

For example, Keith Grand was very keen on horse racing and the race day specials from Paddington to Newbury and Cheltenham were always hauled by the finest steam motive power that Old Oak Common possessed. Never mind that during the second half of the 1950s the WR consistently attained no better annual passenger train punctuality figures than 50 to 60%!

In the Commission's view, the main focus should be accelerating the implementation of the Plan; inflation, a drop in coal and steel traffic and the time needed to win approval for rates increases, which were causing the growing losses, were outside BTC control. Outsiders clamoured for figures to demonstrate financial viability but the Commission lacked the wherewithal to provide these. Those actually produced were seen as of little value when put through forensic scrutiny.

In its 1959 reappraisal the Commission forecast an operating surplus by 1963, later than forecast in the 1956 White Paper. Whereas in the last four years total route miles had only been cut by 300 to 18,850, this was expected to be shaved by 10% between 1959 and 1963. One route that was earmarked for the axe was the Settle & Carlisle, if electrification of the West Coast line to Carlisle could be pushed through.

The White Paper delineated work done and work planned. Ten years after nationalisation, connections between former LNER and LMSR lines around Edinburgh were to provide better routing for mineral traffic. Iron ore shipments between the Midlands and South Wales were to be made over a new route by installing connections between former LMS and GW lines at Fenny Compton and Stratford-upon-Avon, so avoiding 27 miles via Hatton and the need for assistance up the bank there. In South Wales, a new marshalling yard at Margam and the installation of eight miles of colour-light signalling between Pyle and Briton Ferry was to lead to the closure of four yards and nine signalboxes.

Across the network, track relaying would be done with a view to higher speeds and line utilisation, with long-welded rail easing maintenance and it would be being laid at the rate of 320 track miles annually by 1963.

At long last, there was to be a rationalisation of workshop facilities. After the 1923 Grouping, the Big Four did little to rationalise the facilities they had inherited. Of 22 works engaged in locomotive repairs in 1959, only 12 were expected to be so engaged by 1963 and similar steps were to affect carriage and wagon establishments.

Electrification of the Euston line to Liverpool and Manchester was to be completed by 1964, two years earlier than predicted in the 1956 White Paper. This was to be achieved by a concentration of resources on the scheme, to the detriment of the Great Northern line from King's Cross to Hitchin and Letchworth which would now take until 1964. Extension to Leeds and York would be after that date.

The reappraisal predicted that, by 1961, the number of steam locomotives would be 7,800, down from 18,500 at the start of the Plan. This had been the forecast number by 1970 when the Plan was being formulated and shows how steam's elimination was progressing. This did not mean modernisation was delivering the predicted returns, as noted by Chairman Robertson in February

1961. Area Boards were asked to scrutinise all the finished projects, in addition to the detailed financial back-check, to assess the return on the investment.

It is difficult to assess whether forecasts for return on capital for any given project were achieved because of inadequate figures. An added complication was the BTC's use of 'betterment', a term lacking measurable results, and how it was derived. It is also not now possible to fathom how the returns on capital were split between betterment and non-betterment.

Some early schemes included a value for assets that were not life-expired but were to be written off; this practice seemed to cease as time went on. Failing to include within the cost of a scheme the value of assets written off overstates the true return on the new investment. For example, anyone considering replacing a car does not treat the value of the car being replaced as zero, rather its value is a key component in the replacement decision.

Kingmoor yard at Carlisle was estimated to cost £4.8 million and yield a return of 11.3% in total or 13.4% on betterment. By 1962 the cost estimate had risen to £5.4 million but gross and betterment returns were still given as 9.4% and 12% respectively. Despite these questionable financial returns, in August 1960 this project was the largest put before the Ministerial Committee on Modernisation as a sure-fire winner!

The projected return on Ripple Lane yard was 4 to 5%, so not really covering the cost of the capital borrowed to finance it. The ill-starred outer-London freight route was also never expected to show a direct financial return on £11.7 million of investment.

No figures were produced to show whether the traffic handled by these and other new yards was profitable; the overall freight performance after 1956 was in deficit for years. Professional railway managers failed to grasp the situation, and failed to devise a freight strategy before committing funds to projects that they had probably always dreamed about. New yard construction was halted, but not before millions had been wasted on facilities that never achieved their planned potential. It has been estimated that the new Kingmoor yard never bettered two-thirds of its potential capacity. This failure meant they also never produced the forecast return on capital, making them a waste of money to a greater or lesser degree.

When a traffic study was carried out in 1961, it revealed wagon utilisation was still dreadful. The average time lapse between a wagon being loaded and the cycle recommencing was 11.9 days; 1½ to 2 days was spent between loading and unloading, whilst the average transit was 67 miles. It was hardly surprising the lorries, whose drivers could legally work 11 hours a day, were far more competitive.

The demise of the traditional cargo docks at ports such as Liverpool and London in favour of container shipments is further evidence of how the movement of freight changed during the period.

Another failing of merchandise modernisation was the deliberate policy of building new short-wheelbase vehicles, contrary to Continental practice. Modern traction was able to speed up services but several serious derailments established that short-wheelbase wagons were unsuitable for speeds above 55mph, and this imposed a constraint on reducing transit times. In 1955 it should have been evident to the planners that freight rolling stock was the worst in the world among developed countries. Millions were then thrown away on building short-wheelbase wagons with vacuum brakes that were unsuitable for a modern railway.

Another big problem is being confident about any of the traffic data, both volume and value. Figures were out-of-date or too optimistic. Kingmoor Yard's proposal in 1959 was based on 1957 traffic levels, yet it must have been evident when the scheme was being worked up that volumes were in decline. Even when the volume fall was evident in 1962, the requisite 'back-check' only cut the estimated return by 5%.

In 1960 Kent Coast electrification was expected to yield a betterment of only 5%, with net revenue rising from £0.5 million to £3 million and with assets of £33 million in the Commission's accounts written off. Presented with these returns, an MoT working group was critical that the scheme had gone ahead and, in light of this, the Minister stopped the GN suburban electrification scheme out of King's Cross.

Finally, the 'back-check' carried out in 1961 for North Wales dieselisation, introduced in 1955, showed that a forecast 76% betterment had merely reduced a loss of £109,200 using steam to £28,000 by DMU, so still a loss, and this before central charges and interest were included!

Changing times

The five-year period from 1958 was one of turmoil for the railways. Its profitable mineral traffic had gone into long-term decline; it could, or would not see that most of merchandise business was loss-making and no amount of investment would change that; and it believed that a modern freight service would win back traffic that it was proposing to carry at loss-making rates. Chairman Robertson, and his successor Richard Beeching, held low opinions of most senior railway managers and the situation elucidated throughout this book shows why.

Robertson had predicted railway finances would be turned round by 1962, then 1963. In fact, the 1962 accounts revealed an overall deficit of £159 million, a sum on a par with the previous and immediately succeeding years.

What could not be foreseen at the time was that there was no prospect of making the railways break even by the 1960s but the Government, supported by the public, was tired of mounting losses and judged that public money would be better spent on schools, hospitals and a modern network of trunk roads called motorways.

The BTC's cause had not been helped by criticisms within the report of the Parliamentary Select Committee on the Nationalised Industries on the railways and the MoT's own reviews, both coming in 1960. In addition to setting up a Special Advisory Group to consider the railways in general, Minister Ernest Marples had excluded modernisation from that Group's brief and formed the Ministerial Group on Modernisation, which he chaired; Ratter and Grand represented the Commission.

Having lost patience with the existing setup, Marples decided to replace Robertson as Chairman with Beeching from June 1961 and to pass a Transport Act in 1962 which broke up the BTC and created the British Railways Board. The Area Boards set up under the 1953 Act were swept away and power was wielded centrally by the BRB in a reflection of the days of the old RE. Beeching's remit, however, remained the same as in the 1947 Act that BR must pay its way.

Affirming a situation that has been illustrated in Chapter 10, Beeching felt there was inadequate control of investment expenditure and this was but one area where his broom made sweeping changes. Beeching's 1963 report on reshaping the railways was a direct result of Commission failings since 1948. More information about this can be found in the author's book *Dr Beeching's Remedy – A Cure For A Century Of Railway Ills*. Planning for modernisation was to be revised again.

The Modernisation Plan was to be delivered over a 15-year term and it is fair to say that the railways looked markedly different by the latter part of the 1960s when compared to 1955. Train services were cleaner, faster and more punctual. Route rationalisation of passenger operations was about to be dealt with properly. Financial losses were still being incurred despite agreed Government subsidy for socially-necessary routes. There was a dubious legacy in respect of the diesel locomotive fleet and a serious weeding-out process of unreliable types was in progress, made possible by reduced traffic levels. Some locomotives had active lives as short as two years but the debt burden by which they had been financed lived on to some degree.

Not everything had been modernised. Some stations were still lit by Victorian gas lamps in the 1970s! There was a blanket 75mph speed limit across the ScR because of inadequate braking distances between distant and home signals, a legacy from before railway Grouping in 1923. Clearly, there was still more to do.

In conclusion

Clearly, the Modernisation Plan can be judged in different ways. Did it provide improved services for the railway's customers? Did it make the railways more viable? Did the investment yield the predicted returns? Could the railways have survived through the 1960s and 1970s without it? Could it have been implemented better?

The preceding chapters have provided a basis for the reader to draw conclusions because there are so many variables in play. For sure, the services that survived the 1960s were superior to those prior to 1955. When modern operating methods finally worked through, these certainly delivered efficiency gains. Evidence the world over proves that the replacement of steam was correct.

Reading the BTC files, one is struck by the perceptiveness of H. P. Barker, the industrialist and part-time Commission Member. Time and again, his insights into railway operation proved far superior to the collective wisdom of the life-long professional railwaymen at the pinnacle of their careers, the latter often coming across as lacklustre plodders who failed to understand they were running a business.

This may seem a harsh view, but when Fred Margetts was newly promoted from Regional Manager of the NER to the Commission as Member responsible for operations, he was asked to present a paper on Organising the Railway as a Business to a conference of top railway managers in 1962. He admitted that he had never before considered that the railway *was* a business!

It must be fair to conclude that one of the failings with the Plan was much of the thinking behind it, notably solving yesterday's problems rather than being visionary on services and facilities for the future.

The Commission itself must carry a large share of the blame for errors in Plan implementation, most notably the headlong rush to get schemes up and running in order to reap cost savings and so reduce the BTC's financial deficit.

At the annual general meeting of the Southern Railway in 1947, the chairman said the great need was for better co-ordination of transport and that this was a generally-held view. Despite being created in 1948 as the overlord of inland transport, no attempt was made to co-ordinate bus and rail services. Both operated independently, even in competition, with no thought as to cost. In 1956, the WR acknowledged that its timetable carried no information about inter-regional services, nor the principal trains on other Regions, yet there was supposed to be only one railway.

The Select Committee criticised the lack of financial accountability by the Regions, which should have been made to live within balanced budgets. Cost control at all levels was one of the first areas tackled by Chairman Beeching. He introduced structured management training and new brooms at the top within the BRB. At last a modernised way of thinking about railways developed and it became possible to see where losses were being incurred, even if it took time to deal with the situation.

Organisational modernisation only began to take root when the concept of mixed-traffic motive power ended around 1970, passenger and freight managers ploughing their own furrows. Attempts to dispense with Divisions within Regions during the 1970s foundered on management intransigence and it was not until BR was divided into business sectors in the 1980s that Regional boundaries which dated back to a large degree to 1923 finally disappeared. At last, BR began to operate fully on a functional basis, with strict cost accountability. The result might not have pleased enthusiasts but, after all, BR was a business-driven transport undertaking and not a giant, sentimental train set!

Bibliography

Books

Clough, David N., *BR Standard diesels of the 1960s*, Ian Allan

Clough, David N., *Dr Beeching's Remedy, a cure for a century of railway ills*, Ian Allan 2013

Clough, David N., *Hydraulic vs Electric, the battle for the BR diesel fleet*, Ian Allan

Cock, C. M., *The Deltic Locomotive*, The Institution of Electrical Engineers, April 1959

Cox, E. S., *Locomotive Panorama Volume 2*, Ian Allan, 1974

Freeman Allen, G., *British Railways Today and Tomorrow Third Edition*, Ian Allan 1962

Gourvish, Terry, *British Railways 1948-73: A Business History*

Green-Hughes, Evan, *Lightweight DMUs*, Ian Allan 2012

Green-Hughes, Evan, *BR First Generation Diesel Railbuses*, Ian Allan 2013

Haresnape, Brian, *BR Fleet Survey, Parts 1 to 11*, Ian Allan

Harris, Roger, *The Allocation History of BR Diesels & Electrics*, Roger Harris

Webb, B. & Duncan J., *AC Electric Locomotives of British Rail*, David & Charles 1979

Periodicals and technical papers

Issues of *Modern Railways, Railway Gazette, Trains Illustrated*

Sykes, W. J. A., *Operating experience with the diesel-electric train sets on the Hastings services of the Southern Region*, Proceedings of the Institution of Locomotive Engineers, 1960.

Websites

Cousins, Jeff, *Kent Coast Electrification*, Southern Electric Group, www.southernelectric.org.uk/features/historical-features/kentcoast.html

List of tables

No	Description	Page
1	Pre-nationalisation types built after nationalisation	35
2	BR Standard designs	36
3	1953 development programme for BR	43
4	Motive power transition to 1970	50
5	Pilot Scheme orders	77
6	Electric Pilot Scheme orders	99
7	Electric locomotive details	99
8	WR diesel locomotive requirements for combined Areas 1 and 2	130
9	Tenders for second batch of Type 3s for SR	134
10	Main line diesel deliveries 1957 to 1968	142

Index

Advantages of diesel over steam   79

Barker, H. P.,   42, 55-6, 60, 61, 62, 70, 96, 111, 145, 154, 167
Beeching, Dr R.,   20, 56, 84, 149, 150, 165, 166, 168
Bonavia, Michael   28, 29, 31, 44, 46, 81
Bond, R. C.,   19, 20, 28, 44, 46, 65 et seq, 70, 74

Container and roadrailer trains   152-3
Cox, E. S.,   21, 27-9, 31, 69, 70, 107, 126, 126, 127, 137

Design Panel   104, 107 et seq, 120
Diesel Multiple Unit Main Line Express Committee   117
Diesel railcars and DMUs
    Birmingham Area scheme   84-5
    Blue Pullman sets   108, 111 et seq, 149
    Bristol Area scheme   85-7
    Class 123 'Inter City'   121 et seq
    Class 124 'Trans Pennine'   119 et seq
    Derby Lightweight sets   38-9, 80, 81, 91
    Derby St Pancras suburban   82
    GWR   22, 28,37
    LMSR   22
    Metropolitan Cammell   38, 111, 118
    Railbuses   83 et seq
    SR DEMUs   87 et seq
    Swindon First Generation Inter City sets   40-2, 81, 113, 121
Diesel shunters   22, 44
Diesel versus Elecric   137

Electric multiple units (EMUs)
    Class 303   105, 106
    Class 304   100

Class 411   102
Class 414   102
Electrification, forms of: 16, 21-2, 56, 93 et seq
Electrification schemes:
  ECML   50, 56, 60
  Glasgow suburban   48, 50, 58, 96, 104, 162
  Lancaster, Morecambe   16, 106
  London, Enfield, Chingford   16, 50, 60, 106
  London Great Northern outer suburban   16, 28, 50, 60, 163, 165
  London, Tilbury, Southend   15, 50, 60, 96, 162
  Manchester, Sheffield, Wath   14, 15, 16, 22, 25-6
  SR lines in Eastern and Central Divisions   50, 101 et seq, 106, 165
  WCML   56 60, 96 et seq, 106, 147-8, 162, 163

Freight train braking   52, 153-4

Grand, Keith   69, 75, 107, 126, 162, 166

Harrington Committee   28, 29

Inglis report   39-40, 60, 104

Lightweight Trains Committee   29, 37, 40, 83, 84
Locomotives
  6701   26
  10000/1   22-3, 24, 32
  10100   23
  10201-3   23-4, 32
  10800   23, 24, 76
  18000, 18100   24-5, 100
  20001-3   25
  BR Standard steam designs   27-31, 35, 37, 40, 47, 127
  Class 14   131-2, 140-1
  Class 21   138-9
  Class 22   70, 72, 160
  Class 23   72, 139
  Class 24   107
  Class 28   76
  Class 33   103, 134

Class 35   130-1
Class 40   72, 75, 76-8, 129, 153
Class 41   70, 72, 74
Class 42   74-6, 129
Class 43   75
Class 44   72, 76=78
Class 47   108, 109, 131, 136, 153
Class 52   109, 129-31
Class 55   109, 110, 126, 129, 132-3
Class 71   102
Class 73   103
Class 76   26
Class 94xx 0-6-0PTs   30, 74
Class 'Leader'   25
DB Class V200   69, 70, 71, 74, 75
Deltic   71, 72, 126, 132
E1000, E2001   100
Electric Pilot Scheme   97 et seq, 106
Locomotive exchange trials 1948   27, 30
Locomotive Manufacturers Association   49, 72, 75

Marples, Ernest   160, 166
Marshalling yards   150, 159, 160, 163, 164, 165
Merry-go-round trains   152

Phillips, H. H.,   45, 46, 69, 74, 117
Pilot Scheme for diesels locomotives   49, 56, 65 et seq, 126 et seq
Pilot Scheme for electric locomotives   97
Planning Committee on modernisation   44 et seq, 55 et seq, 70
Pope, F.,   18, 19, 29, 30,37, 42, 57, 98
Pullman services, Regional attitudes towards   113, 116

Ratter, J.,   19, 20, 42, 45, 81, 138, 166
Riddles, R. A.,   12, 18, 21, 27-33, 3-8
Robertson, Sir Brian   17, 18, 19, 44, 56, 57, 81, 83, 90, 105, 106, 127, 129,
      133, 136, 138, 158, 162, 163, 165, 166

Technical, Research & Development Committee   19, 65, 67, 69, 72, 73, 93,
      95, 96, 98, 100, 103, 106, 111, 119-20, 125, 127, 152, 153

Traffic Costing Service   55, 60, 61
Train heating   73, 97, 139
Train, J. C. L.,   12, 18, 19, 20, 48, 49, 58, 65, 70, 937, 98
Transport Act, 1953   17 et seq, 29

Warder, S. B.,   42, 45, 46, 67, 70, 88, 93, 94, 95, 98
Wilson, Reginald   42, 55, 57, 83
Works & Equipment Committee   19, 40, 65, 69, 70, 71, 72, 76, 78, 80, 89,
     90, 97, 98, 105, 121, 128, 130